Brown
v.
Board of Education
Equal Schooling for All

Harvey Fireside
and
Sarah Betsy Fuller

Landmark Supreme Court Cases

Enslow Publishers, Inc.

40 Industrial Road	PO Box 38
Box 398	Aldershot
Berkeley Heights, NJ 07922	Hants GU12 6BP
USA	UK

http://www.enslow.com

Library of Congress Cataloging-in-Publication Data

Fireside, Harvey.
    Brown v. Board of Education: equal schooling for all / Harvey
Fireside and Sarah Betsy Fuller.
        p. cm.—(Landmark Supreme Court Cases)
    Includes bibliographical references and index.
    ISBN 0-89490-469-8
    1. Brown, Oliver, 1918- —Trials, litigation, etc.—
Juvenile literature. 2. Topeka (Kan.). Board of Education
—Trials, litigation, etc.—Juvenile literature.
3. Segregation in education—Law and legislation—
United States—Juvenile literature.
[1. Segregation in education—Law and legislation. 2. Afro
Americans—Civil rights.] I. Fuller, Sarah Betsy.
II. Title. III. Title: Brown versus Board of Education. IV. Series
KF228.B76F57 1994
344.73'0798—dc20   93-5897
[347.304798]   CIP
                                                       AC

Printed in the United States of America.

10 9

Photo Credits: National Archives, p. 43; New York Public Library, pp. 8, 22, 24, 28, 58, 70, 86; "Photography by Bachrach. Collection of the Supreme Court of the United States," p. 93; "Photography by Harris & Ewing. Collection of the Supreme Court of the United States," pp. 65, 82.

Cover Photo: Franz Jantzen, "Collection of the Supreme Court of the United States" (background); Prints and Photographs Division, Library of Congress (insert).

Contents

To Leela, Douglas and Daniel
—H.F.

To Cecily, Jonah and Gabriel
—S.B.F.

1

Linda Carol Brown Leads the Way

In 1950, eight-year-old Linda Carol Brown discovered she could not attend the Sumner School, even though it was only a ten-minute walk from her home on First Street in Topeka, Kansas. At the time, she could scarcely have imagined that a lawsuit in her name would make United States history.[1]

The Browns, who were African Americans, lived in a mixed ethnic neighborhood near the Sumner School. They had received a notice at their front door telling them how to register their children for fall classes. Linda's father, Oliver, took her to the school and left her outside while he went to the principal's office. When he came out a few minutes later, Linda saw that he was upset.

What the notice didn't say was that the Sumner School was for whites only.[2]

Linda and her two sisters were being kept out of Sumner because Topeka city law set up separate elementary schools for blacks and whites.

As Oliver Brown later told the federal judge who would hear the case, it was dangerous to have Linda travel six blocks on foot through a vast amount of traffic, then take a school bus to the Monroe School reserved for black children.[3] In order for her to go to the school across town, she had to leave her house at 7:40 A.M., walk between the train tracks from the railroad yard on First Street, and wait for the bus. Frequently, the bus was late, leaving her on the corner in the cold, rain, or snow. If the bus came on time, Linda would arrive a half hour before school opened at 9:00 A.M., and be forced to wait outside. She often had to clap her hands or jump up and down to keep warm.[4]

Oliver Brown did not want his child exposed to these hardships. He wanted Linda to be able to go to her neighborhood school, a safe seven-block walk from home. So he decided to fight for her right to do so in the courts.[5] The National Association for the Advancement of Colored People (NAACP) took up Linda's case, together with that of seven other black children, against the Topeka Board of Education. Linda Carol Brown, whose family name was first in alphabetical order, led the way.

One thing Linda remembered later was the time her father took her to the Church of God. The minister asked her to stand up in front of everyone, while he asked, "Why should this child be forced to travel so far to school each day?"[6]

Another father with children in black Topeka Schools was Silas Hardrick Fleming. He had followed Oliver Brown to the witness stand on June 5, 1951, to tell the federal judges how complicated it had become to find bus transportation to the black school, when his children could have walked to a nearby white school. Fleming tried to explain why he had joined the lawsuit, but the lawyer for the school board objected. Silas Fleming hadn't been asked that question. Judge Walter Huxman interrupted, saying to Fleming, "Go ahead and tell the court." He wasn't out to criticize teachers in the black schools, Silas Fleming said, but "I and my children are craving light, the entire colored race is craving light, and the only way to reach the light is to start out children together in their infancy and they come up together."[7]

By the time the case of *Brown* v. *Board of Education of Topeka, Kansas* made its way to the Supreme Court a year later, Linda Carol Brown had been joined by dozens of other children as the plaintiffs, those who bring a lawsuit

An African-American mother tries to enroll her son in a school on Long Island, N.Y., in September of 1964, against white opposition.

because they have been wronged in a case. Kansas had been one of four states that gave individual cities such as Topeka the choice of having integrated (mixed-race) or segregated (separate-race) elementary schools. The Brown case was taken up by the Supreme Court together with four other cases from Delaware, Virginia, South Carolina, and the District of Columbia. In those, as well as fourteen other states, only segregated elementary and high schools were allowed.

In South Carolina, for example, the state constitution stated that "no child of either race shall ever be permitted to attend a school provided for children of the other race."[8] In Topeka, Kansas, the trial court had found the condition of the white and black schools to be "substantially equal." In rural Clarendon County, South Carolina, however, there was no doubt that black schools were markedly inferior. Black children attended run-down, ramshackle schoolhouses, some with just one or two teachers, crowded classrooms, and no libraries, lunchrooms, or playgrounds. Blacks made up 70 percent of the county's population; a third of them grew up illiterate, unable to read or write.[9]

Black children spent only six months of the year in school. They were expected to help their parents farm, so they were taken out of school at planting and harvesting times.[10] Clarendon County spent only $43 per year to educate each black child, compared to $179 per white child.[11]

Levi Pearson was one of the first local black farmers to challenge the system in Clarendon County. His three children, Eloise, age twelve, James, fifteen, and Daisy, eighteen, had to be bused nine miles to their segregated high school in Scott's Branch. The old bus was always breaking down. In 1947, Pearson sued School District 26 for failing to provide adequate bus transportation for his children. But on June 8, 1948, the Charleston court threw out the case based on a procedural technicality, a detail. The Pearson property was right on the line between District 5, where they paid taxes, and District 26, where the children went to school. Pearson was found to lack the legal standing, the right under the law, to bring the case to court.

In March 1949, the Pearsons and a few other black residents of Clarendon County drove to the state capital, Columbia, to talk with officials of the NAACP. They met with Thurgood Marshall, an attorney from the NAACP's New York office who had been winning cases to allow blacks to vote and to attend all-white law schools. Marshall listened to Levi Pearson's story of the troubles he had encountered after filing his lawsuit.[12] Every white-owned bank and store had cut off the Pearsons' credit. He was unable to buy supplies for his farm. When he cut down his trees, the lumber mill refused to pick up the logs. The white businessmen were trying to intimidate, frighten Pearson. They wanted him to drop his lawsuit and to make sure no other black people would fight for integrated, mixed-race schools.

But Thurgood Marshall wanted to make sure that individual blacks would not be intimidated by such tactics, perhaps pressured to drop their suit. Marshall asked for twenty plaintiffs from Clarendon County to file a class action suit. This is a case where many people have the same complaint and take it to court together. If they win, *all* members of the "class" are granted relief. In this case, a victory in court would extend to all black students in the state's segregated schools. It took eight months to find nineteen other plaintiffs to join the Pearsons. By now, the suit had turned away from the issue of better transportation, to the issue of better schools.

The new lawsuit would be headed by Harry Briggs, because his name was first in alphabetical order. Briggs was a Navy veteran with five children. He farmed twenty acres and also worked as a mechanic at a gas station. Soon he felt the community's pressure to drop his complaint. He recalled, "The white folks got kind of sour. They asked me to take my name from the petition."[13]

The white gas station owner asked Harry Briggs if he

knew what he was doing. His answer: "I'm doing if for the benefit of my children." On Christmas Eve, his boss said "Harry, I want me a *boy*—and I can pay him less than you." (Whites called a black man "boy" as an insult.) Harry was fired.[14]

Mrs. Briggs had been working as a chambermaid at a motel in Summerton. She was asked to persuade her husband to drop the suit. When she said she wouldn't, she was told this was her last week at her job. Other black parents who had participated in the suit also found themselves out of work and pushed off their farmlands.[15]

Yet in 1951, a three-judge federal court heard the case of *Briggs* v. *Elliot*. (R.W. Elliot was the Clarendon County school official.)

Thurgood Marshall's legal strategy had been three-pronged. First, he wanted to establish the obvious difference in quality between the black and white schools of Clarendon County. Second, he was out to challenge the constitutionality of the South Carolina laws decreeing segregation. He wanted to show that they violated the Fourteenth Amendment of the United States Constitution, which guarantees "equal protection of the laws" to all. Third, he brought experts like Dr. Kenneth Clark, a psychology professor at City College of New York, to testify on the harmful effects of segregation. Dr. Clark had given the black children at Scott's Branch his "doll test." Two-thirds of them chose a white doll as the "nice" one, the black twin doll as the "bad" one. This showed, said Dr. Clark, that segregated schools caused a black child to have "basic feelings of inferiority, conflict, confusion in his self-image."[16] Nonetheless, a majority of the court decided that the state law was constitutional.

The opinion, written by Judge John J. Parker, said that the schools would soon be equal. He believed that any differences between the black and white schools would disappear because the state lawmakers had just passed a $75 million school bond issue.[17] Governor James F. (Jimmy) Byrnes said that most of that money would be spent on improving the quality of black schools. The governor's promise satisfied the court. The court gave Clarendon County six months to report what progress had been made in bringing black schools up to the level of white ones. If the system of segregation was ever to change, Judge Parker said, "This is a matter for the legislature [state lawmakers] and not the courts."[18]

Only the third judge, J. Waties Waring, wrote a stinging dissent, or opinion in disagreement. Judge Waring said, "Segregation in education can never produce equality and is an evil that must be eradicated . . . . The system of segregation in education adopted and practiced in the state of South Carolina must go and must go now. *Segregation is per se inequality.*"[19] (In other words, separating black school children by law made them feel inferior.)

In the nation's capital, Gardner Bishop, a barber, had led repeated attempts to integrate the schools of Washington, D.C. On September 11, 1950, he brought a group of eleven children to the brand-new John Philip Sousa Junior High School, across from a golf course in the southeast section of the city. This school had a 600-seat auditorium, a playground with seven basketball courts, and 42 sparkling new classrooms.

When Bishop tried to enroll the children, pointing out that Sousa Junior High had several empty classrooms, he was turned away. The principal refused to accept the black children.[20] Next, Bishop took his group to the city's board of education. Here, too, the superintendent of schools explained that he was just following the laws that the Congress had passed for the District of Columbia. John Philip Sousa Junior High School was for whites only. [21]

Gardner Bishop was not satisfied and started to look for an attorney to help the children go to the best school available.[22]

Meanwhile, they had to start their school year, once again, at all-black schools. One of the boys, Spottswood Bolling, Jr., went back to Shaw Junior High School, a 46-year-old building in a run-down section of

Washington. Bishop found an attorney named James Madison Nabrit, Jr., to argue the case. The Bolling name led off the lawsuit, *Bolling* v. *Sharpe*, directed at C. Melvin Sharpe, the president of the District of Columbia board of education.

Nabrit, who argued the case in early 1951 for the black children in the United States District Court, was a professor of law at Howard University and an adviser to the NAACP Legal Defense Fund.

He focused on the question of whether the district government could show that it made sense to set up segregated schools. He asked two questions: Were segregated schools reasonable, and did they fulfill a public purpose? He cited the history of the school system to show that segregation was both *unreasonable* and of no benefit to the community.[23]

As our nation's capital, the District of Columbia was governed directly by the Congress of the United States. After the Civil War, Nabrit argued, if Congress had wanted to, it could have set up a completely segregated school system. Since it had not done so, the later acts of Congress establishing separate schools were *bills of attainder,* that is, unconstitutional actions that "inflict punishment without a judicial trial."[24] The black children who tried to attend white schools in the district were being punished because of their skin color and denied their basic rights, Nabrit said. "What schooling was good enough to meet their constitutional rights 160 or 80 years ago [when the Bill of Rights and the Fourteenth Amendment had been passed] is different from the question of what schooling meets their rights now."[25] The bill of attainder argument might seem far fetched, but it was one of the few clauses in the Constitution that Nabrit could use against the federal government. The "equal protection" clause of the Fourteenth Amendment could be applied only to state actions.

Judge Walter M. Bastian, of the United States District Court, ruled against Spottswood Bolling and the other children in April 1951. He said there was nothing he could do. Since the black children had not established the inferiority of their schools, he could not order the schools to be improved, as judges had in various states. Here, in the District of Columbia, blacks did have adequate schools to attend. The Supreme Court precedents, going back to 1896, approved segregated schools; thus, Judge Bastian said he would not go against the expressed will of Congress.[26]

James Nabrit was dissatisfied with that decision.[27] Since he had lost the trial in the United States District Court, he could take the case to a Circuit Court of Appeals; then, if he lost again, he could ask the United

States Supreme Court to decide the case. He started preparing his case for the United States Court of Appeals. But the Supreme Court stepped in. By 1952, the mood of the country had changed. All of these lawsuits had exposed the injustice of segregated education for black students. The Supreme Court, the highest court in the land, needed to decide once and for all whether "separate but equal" schools anywhere in the country were legal under the Constitution.

So the Supreme Court decided to hear *Bolling* v. *Sharpe* together with Linda Brown's Case from Kansas and others from Delaware, Virginia, and South Carolina. Linda Carol Brown's fight had made it to the Supreme Court of the United States. The Court relied on a seldom-used rule for cases "of such imperative public importance as to justify the deviation from normal appellate processes and to require immediate settlement in this Court." In other words, the Supreme Court skipped the U.S. Court of Appeals and took the cases (which were all treated as one) from Washington, D.C., directly.

2

The Walls of Separation Begin to Crumble

Since 1619, blacks had been brought to this country as slaves. Their white owners bought and sold them, mainly in the South, to work the fields. To justify the inhumane practice of slavery, the slave owners believed that they themselves were superior.[1] They did not allow the slaves to become educated, and even stopped them from reading the Bible. The few who did learn to read and write had to do so in secret, to escape punishment.

The slaves were freed during the Civil War, through President Lincoln's "Emancipation Proclamation" in 1863 and by the Thirteenth Amendment added to the Constitution in 1865. At last they could satisfy their thirst for learning. The freed blacks flocked to the schools and, for a few years after the Civil War, they attended schools together with whites. Their rights were protected until 1876 by northern Union army troops who occupied the South under a postwar plan called Reconstruction.

The exact history of integration varied from place to place. In New Orleans, for example, whites had resisted at first by placing their children in segregated private schools. A court order, however, ordered the integration of all public schools in 1870. The New Orleans parents and schools had to accept the court order. By 1875, public schools were enrolling 21,000 white and 5,000 black children; the number of white students in private schools had dropped to 14,000.[2]

Why did the New Orleans community send black and white students to school together for several years, without any violent protest? Historians believe that the leaders of the white community accepted integration because they needed the votes of the black citizens to get rid of government agents from the North, known as "carpetbaggers" (who arrived with large suitcases made from squares of carpet).[3] The city government also tried to satisfy demands of the black citizens for economic reasons. The white merchants relied on business from black customers.

But in December of 1874, a group known as the

19

White League took command of the New Orleans public schools. Its members resented the rules imposed by the North; they invaded the schools that had been integrated and threw out the black children bodily. Some of the children returned, however, and integration of a sort lasted for another two and a half years in the city. In other parts of the South, as well, radical groups of white citizens put an end to the period known as Reconstruction in which blacks had been accepted as having equal rights.[4]

In 1876, there was a dispute about who had won the election for president of the United States. It appeared that the Republican candidate Rutherford B. Hayes, had lost the election to the Democrat, Samuel J. Tilden. But the votes of three southern states—Florida, Louisiana, and South Carolina—were in doubt. Congress set up a commission to decide which candidate had won the three states, and the Republican members made a deal with the southern representatives. The three states would award Hayes the votes he needed to win, and he would then withdraw northern troops from the South. Part of the deal was that Hayes promised he would not enforce the Fifteenth Amendment, adopted in 1870. This guaranteed the freed blacks the right to vote.[5] In March 1877, the commission declared Hayes the winner, although he had received 250,000 fewer votes than Tilden.

The agreement with Hayes meant the end of Reconstruction; now southern states could deprive blacks of their right to vote without interference from Washington, D.C. Mississippi, for example, drew up a new constitution in 1890 that effectively disenfranchised blacks and kept them from voting. It required voters to pay poll taxes, fees to be allowed to vote, to pass literacy and "good character" tests, and set up primary elections in which only whites were permitted to vote. "Grandfather clauses" made it possible to avoid taking the tests if one's grandfather had voted. No blacks could take advantage of this, however, because they were the first generation to vote.[6] Throughout the South, the former slave owners and other whites were determined to deny blacks full citizenship.

By the 1890s, all eleven southern states were adopting laws that put up barriers to keep black citizens not only out of schools reserved for whites but also out of libraries, hospitals, parks, theaters, trains, and hotels. These racist laws made blacks feel inferior, because they were denied their basic human rights. Even toilets and drinking fountains were marked "White Only" and "Colored." Until the 1960s, "colored" and "Negro" were the terms

One of the signs of "Jim Crow" segregation in the South. The "Colored Balcony" of the movie theater is clearly marked, to separate blacks from whites.

regularly used for people who today call themselves African American or black.

It was evident to black citizens that their separate places to eat, sleep, or travel were in much worse shape than those reserved for whites. But the southern whites who had regained power pretended that the separate services for blacks were equal to those of whites. Thus, Louisiana had passed a law in 1890 that required railroads to offer "separate but equal accommodations for the white and colored races," though in practice first-class carriages were set aside solely for white passengers.[7] It wasn't just a question of cleaner and more comfortable cars being reserved for whites, but of the shame that blacks felt being allowed to use only the so-called Jim Crow cars. Jim Crow was an insulting term for blacks, taken from a minstrel show character of the same name.[8] In 1891, a group of Creoles, people of mixed white and black ancestry, formed a "Citizens' Committee to Test the Constitutionality of the Separate Car Law."

In order to do this, someone would deliberately break the law and get arrested. The Creoles hoped that they could then prove in court that the law should not be upheld because it violated the Constitution.[9] On June 7, 1892, a Creole named Homer A. Plessy, who was light-skinned and described himself as "seven-eighths

Before integration, black schools in the South were crowded into one room and poorly equipped.

Caucasian," took his seat in the first-class carriage for which he had bought a ticket in New Orleans. When asked, he refused to move to the coach set aside for blacks. The conductor called the police, and Plessy was arrested and taken to jail. He was then scheduled for trial by Judge John H. Ferguson, but he appealed Judge Ferguson's order to the Louisiana Supreme Court, which ruled against Plessy.

By 1896, the case known as *Plessy* v. *Ferguson* had reached the United States Supreme Court. To the dismay of black Americans, seven of the nine Supreme Court justices upheld the "separate but equal" law of Louisiana. One of them didn't participate and one dissented, or disagreed with the majority. Justice Henry Billings Brown spoke for the Court. That law was not in violation of the Fourteenth Amendment, he said, because it only guaranteed the *political* equality of Negroes, not their *social* equality. The government, said Justice Brown, was powerless to end separation of "the two races in schools, theaters, and railway carriages." If such segregation were to be overcome, it had to be by the "voluntary consent of individuals," not by legislation that was "powerless to eradicate social instincts." Indeed, claimed Justice Brown, if blacks like Homer Plessy felt inferior in their separate cars, it wasn't the fault of the law but their own fault, because they "chose to put that construction on it."[10]

Not so, protested Justice John Marshall Harlan in a lone, angry dissent. The Louisiana law "puts the brand of servitude and degradation upon a large class of our fellow citizens, our equals before the law," said Justice Harlan. The injustice wasn't only in the minds of blacks, as the majority of the Court had held. It was the state's flagrant discrimination, "wholly inconsistent with the civil freedom and the equality before the law established by the Constitution." Such a system of separating citizens by skin color, said Justice Harlan, was trying to set up whites as a "superior, dominant, ruling class of citizens," or a "caste." And that was specifically prohibited by law, since "our Constitution is color blind" and "All citizens are equal before the law."[11]

The *Plessy* decision put the stamp of approval of the Supreme Court on segregation throughout the South. The impact of the case went far beyond separate railroad cars. The Court's opinion, for example, had given its approval also to segregated public schools set up by Congress in the District of Columbia "as well as by the legislatures of many of the states." Separate schools for black and white children now spread not only through the South but also to some border states, like Delaware, and even to areas of the North, including parts of Kansas.

It would take another sixty years before the United States Supreme Court was ready to listen to what had been the lonely dissenting voice of Justice Harlan.

Many blacks left the South during the early years of the twentieth century. More than a million blacks joined the "Great Migration" north between 1910 and 1930.[12] Although there was discrimination against them in the North as well—in schools and housing and in the workplace—at least, there, blacks were able to vote. In the cotton economy of the South, most blacks were tenant framers or sharecroppers. They were never permitted to own their land, and much of the little they earned they had to pay back to their white landlords. In the North, blacks began to be elected to public office in Chicago, Detroit, Cleveland, Philadelphia, and New York City, even to Congress. During the 1920s, black writers contributed to the flowering of poetry and novels in a cultural movement known as the "Harlem Renaissance." The Harlem Renaissance was a show of black pride expressed in art, music, and literature by blacks in New York City.

The remaining 9 million blacks stayed in the South, about three-fourths of them in rural areas, farming land that belonged to whites.[13] They were subject to extreme laws and officially tolerated violence. In Alabama, for example, blacks and whites were not legally allowed even

27

Southern blacks waiting to go north. About 1.5 million blacks left to look for better job opportunities between 1910 and 1930.

to play checkers together! In Mississippi, blacks and whites had to use separate telephone booths. In Florida and North Carolina, white children could not touch textbooks that had been used by black students. By 1916, the eleven southern states spent on the education of a black child about one-fourth of the amount allotted to a white child.

Worst of all, a black man growing up in the South had to live with the fear of being lynched, or tortured and murdered without trial, by a white mob—for something he was believed to have said or done to challenge the system of injustice. At the beginning of the twentieth century, more than a hundred black men were brutally lynched each year. No southern policeman stood up to the white mobs, and no one was ever arrested for these murders until 1918 (when fifteen whites were convicted in Winston-Salem, North Carolina, for attempting to lynch an innocent black man).[14] Often the killers wore the hoods and white sheets of the Ku Klux Klan to hide their identity and to spread terror in the black community. But the United States Congress never passed a law making lynching a federal crime. Attempts to do so were filibustered, talked to death, in the Senate.[15]

Except for an Anti-Lynching League, organized by Ida B. Wells, an African-American teacher, writer, and speaker from Mississippi, there were few civil rights organizations. And speakers against lynchings found more support in Europe than in the United States. One of the first black political groups was launched by a brilliant black educator, W.E.B. Du Bois, in 1905: the Niagara Movement, named after its first session, held on the Canadian side of Niagara Falls.

Du Bois, the first black man to earn a Ph.D. degree from Harvard University, had taken issue with Booker T. Washington, the leading black spokesman of the time. Washington used to tell "colored men to be patient," and to avoid "political agitation." He asked black workers to "learn to dignify and glorify common labor" and to pursue vocational education.[16] Du Bois, on the other hand, called for an end to discrimination in the South. He wanted blacks to demand their right to vote and to set their sights on higher education.[17]

Mary White Ovington was a white social worker and writer who had reported on the Niagara Movement. She agreed that "the spirit of the abolitionists must be revived," to get rid of the new forms of slavery imposed on black citizens.[18] Ms. Ovington met with Dr. Henry Moskowitz, a social worker, and William English Walling, a southerner who had written about the 1908 riots in Springfield, Illinois, the former home of Lincoln, which had experienced two especially brutal lynchings.

With financial support from Oswald Garrison Villard, president of the New York *Evening Post,* they agreed to print a call for a national conference, which would bring three hundred white and black leaders together in New York on May 31, 1909.[19] Du Bois addressed the meeting on the "new slavery" of blacks in the South, deprived of the right to vote, limited to vocational schools, and denied their civil liberties.

By the time of its second conference a year later, the group established itself under a new name, the National Association for the Advancement of Colored People (NAACP). It would quickly grow into the most powerful civil rights organization in the country. The only black among the group's officers was Du Bois, as director of publicity and research. He devoted much of his energy to editing a new monthly journal, called *The Crisis.* Starting with a first edition of a thousand copies in November 1910, it reached a hundred thousand ten years later, and it remained the leading Negro magazine for twenty-five years.

The NAACP answered a national need; it had grown to fifty branches by the end of 1914, after its attorneys had begun to win legal victories. Earlier that year, they were able to get the Supreme Court to overturn an Oklahoma voting law excusing whites, whose grandfathers had been voters, from having to take a literacy test (in *Guinn* v. *United States*).[20] This practice was known as a grandfather clause. In 1917, another NAACP suit won a decision against a law in Louisville, Kentucky, that barred blacks from living in blocks occupied by a majority of whites. The case was known as *Buchanan* v. *Warley*.[21]

In 1930, the NAACP decided to challenge segregation in southern schools. Charles Houston, dean of the Howard University Law School, became the association's new legal director in 1935. The following year he hired a former student of his named Thurgood Marshall to bring legal action against states, such as Georgia and South Carolina, that offered no graduate education to blacks. In 1938, the NAACP persuaded the Supreme Court to overturn a Missouri ruling that a black man named Lloyd Gaines must be sent to a law school out of state, rather than admitted to the state's own school. This case was known as *Missouri ex rel. Gaines* v. *Canada*.[22] *Ex rel.* stands for "ex relatione," or "in the name of." It is used for a case in which the state's attorney general presents the suit of a private person—here Gaines, against S.W. Canada, registrar of the University of Missouri. Chief Justices Charles Evans Hughes pointed out that such discrimination violated the "equal protection" clause of the Fourteenth Amendment, because in Missouri only "a Negro resident" was forced to "go outside the state to obtain" his law degree.

On October 11, 1939, the NAACP set up a separate Legal Defense and Educational Fund, Inc. "to render free legal aid to Negroes who suffer legal injustice because of their race."[23] Unlike its parent NAACP, this Legal Defense Fund (for short) would not take a political stand, lobbying for special laws, so that it could attract donations under the new tax laws as a "nonprofit organization." Thurgood Marshall directed this fund in his capacity as the NAACP's Special Counsel. Throughout the 1930s he and the other fund lawyers had been concentrating on insisting on "separate but equal" schooling under the *Plessy* formula, to bring black schools up to the level of their white counterparts.

But after World War II ended in 1945 the mood of the country changed. Black men had served in the armed forces, though often doing menial jobs, and many more had gone north to work in defense industries. They were determined not to forget about the war's promises to spread democracy.[24] A new president, Harry S. Truman, appointed a committee of blacks and whites that recommended the end of segregation, especially in higher education. President Truman also abolished racial quotas in the Army in 1949. Within a year black and white soldiers were fighting side by side in the Korean War. In

33

that new national mood, Thurgood Marshall decided it was not enough merely to ask for black access to separate schools.[25] In its new strategy, the NAACP would do legal battle head-on with the *Plessy* decision. The goal was a fully integrated school system, from law schools to kindergartens.[26]

3

The Case for Linda Brown and Others

When Thurgood Marshall was growing up, it would have been hard to predict that he would head the legal team that succeeded in having the Supreme Court open schoolhouse doors to millions of black children. Marshall was born on July 2, 1908, in West Baltimore, Maryland, to a father who worked as a waiter on railroad dining cars and a mother who taught in a segregated elementary school. The courses he chose in high school seemed to show that he apparently agreed to his mother's wish that he grow up to be a dentist.[1]

As a teenager, he took a job with his father during vacations, as a waiter on the Baltimore & Ohio Railroad. When he first reported to work, the chief dining-car steward gave him his uniform, a white jacket and a black pair of pants that were far too short for the six-foot-tall young man. Marshall asked for a longer pair. "Boy," said the steward, "we can get a shorter Negro to fit these pants a lot easier than we can get new pants to fit you. Why don't you scrunch down a little more?" Marshall needed the job to pay for his education, and as he later recalled, "I scrunched."[2]

In public school, and later in Lincoln University, a college for black men in Pennsylvania, he had a knack for getting into trouble. He cut a lot of his college classes, then spent a good deal of time playing cards. In his sophomore year, he was suspended for hazing new students—shaving their heads so that they could be members of his fraternity. Marshall was known as a playboy, but he settled down to earn a B average, and to receive his degree with honors in 1930. He had decided to study law.

After being turned down by the segregated law school of the University of Maryland, he entered law school at all-black Howard University. So that he could save money by living at home, he got up every day at 5:30 A.M. to catch the train from Baltimore to Washington. His talent as a future lawyer was soon recognized by several of his professors, including William Henry Hastie, who was to become the country's first black federal judge, and by

Charles Hamilton Houston, who later recruited Marshall for work at the NAACP.[3]

Early in his career with the NAACP, Marshall had traveled around the country, constantly responding to requests for legal help from black communities. When it came to fighting for decent schools, Marshall found it exhausting to file suits in each district, in order to raise the quality of black schools to that of the white ones. There were more than 11,000 segregated school districts, mostly in the South, where schools for black children were clearly inferior. White children generally had modern buildings, school buses, sports programs, well paid teachers, and new books and equipment. Black schools were often located in run-down shacks, with inadequate books and supplies, and teachers who were very poorly paid.

The Legal Defense Fund had neither the staff nor the money to handle thousands of lawsuits. But Marshall was able to assemble a staff of able young attorneys who could focus on the four cases from Kansas, Delaware, Virginia, and South Carolina, which the Supreme Court agreed to hear under the umbrella title of *Brown* v. *Board of Education*, plus the fifth case, *Bolling* v. *Sharpe*, which came from the District of Columbia.[4] Marshall was in charge of courtroom strategy. He also argued in person at the Supreme Court, the case against South Carolina, while Robert L. Carter took on Kansas, Spottswood W. Robinson II argued the Virginia suit, Jack Greenberg and Louis L. Reading were assigned to Delaware, and E. C. Hayes and James Nabrit handled the Bolling case against the District of Columbia.[5]

These lawyers had won their biggest victories quite recently in two cases decided by the Supreme Court on the same day, June 5, 1950.[6]

These decisions ruled that, even when states offered nearly identical places to blacks and whites to attend segregated graduate schools, their forced separation deprived blacks of the chance to mingle with the whites with whom they would later have contact. Their degrees from segregated black schools didn't have the prestige of diplomas from the state universities. A unanimous Court agreed that black students confined in the walled-off quarters of their school had been deprived of the "equal protection of the laws" that the Fourteenth Amendment guaranteed. While the justices still claimed that they were not altogether discarding the "separate but equal" rule of the *Plessy* decision, they seemed to reject that rule when it came to higher education.

Later that same year, Thurgood Marshall told the NAACP that "the complete destruction of all enforced segregation is now in sight . . . . Segregation no longer has the stamp of legality in public education."[7] The two

1950 cases had shown to what extremes southern states were willing to go to avoid the physical merging of their universities. In *McLaurin* v. *Oklahoma,* a 68-year-old black professor named George W. McLaurin tried to enroll at the University of Oklahoma for a graduate course in education that was not offered at the state's Negro college, Langston University. The state university admitted McLaurin, after being ordered to do so by a federal court. But university officials asked him to sit in the hall outside the classroom, to study at a special desk behind a screen at the library, and to eat at a separate table in the cafeteria at hours when white students were not using it.[8]

By the time his case was accepted by the Supreme Court, McLaurin had been admitted to the classroom, but behind a rail marked "Reserved for Colored." He was able to eat at common hours in the cafeteria, but still at a separate table. Chief Justice Fred Vinson found that Oklahoma University's restrictions indeed handicapped McLaurin. The school's rules inhibited "his ability to study, to engage in discussion and exchange of views with other students, and, in general, to learn his profession." It wasn't enough to give McLaurin equal treatment—once the school admitted him, "he must receive the same treatment at the hands of the state as students of other races."[9]

In the second case, *Sweatt* v. *Painter*, the Court went even further in stating that separate graduate schools for black students were unequal as such. Heman Marion Sweatt was a postal clerk who had applied to the University of Texas law school because the state had no separate law school for Negroes. When his application was rejected, he sued the university (Theophilus Painter was its president), which then set up a "colored" law school. In its first version, this school consisted of two rented rooms in Houston with two black lawyers as its faculty. When Sweatt sued again, Texas offered three rented rooms across from the state capitol in Austin, with three part-time instructors from the all-white law school.[10] When Thurgood Marshall arrived for Sweatt's trial, he said, "I think we've humored the South long enough . . . This is going to be a real showdown fight against Jim Crow in education."[11]

Nevertheless, the Texas courts ruled against Sweatt, and the NAACP had to wait for the case to reach the Supreme Court to find justice. By this time, Texas had opened a new black law school with five full-time professors and a substantial library; student for student, it rivaled the state's law school for whites in its faculty and books. Even then, said Chief Justice Vinson, speaking for a unanimous Supreme Court, the white school "is superior" in the "numbers of faculty, variety of courses," and other offerings. But beyond that, the "University of Texas law school possesses to a far greater degree those qualities which are incapable of objective measurement but which make for greatness in a law school."[12] In other words, nonphysical features of the school, such as its prestige, the reputation of its teachers, and the influence of its alumni, made it superior.

Lastly, Heman Sweatt would be deprived in the black law school of the chance to have contact with the whites who made up "85 percent of the population of the state" and most of the colleagues with whom he would be dealing when he became a lawyer. Without the learning environment that included white fellow students, Sweatt would be denied his equal right to a "legal education equivalent to that offered by the state to students of other races." As Justice Vinson concluded, Sweatt had to be admitted to the Texas University law school, but the precedent of *Plessy* v. *Ferguson* did not have to be overturned.[13]

It did not seem logical for the Court to state that a segregated school denied black students their basic rights at universities, on the one hand, and then to uphold the *Plessy* rule of "separate but equal" for elementary and high schools, on the other. Stating that contradiction, made up the opening lines of the *Brown* appeal to the Supreme Court. The second approach was to show that

States had fundamentally changed in the sixty years since the *Plessy* decision gave the Court's blessing to a separate (and inferior) place for blacks. Finally, Thurgood Marshall and his associates used the research of psychologists to persuade the Justices that forcing black children to attend segregated schools caused them serious harm.

From the questions that the Justices asked of the Legal Defense Fund lawyers in the *Brown* case, it was clear that most of the Court's members were ready to accept the general idea of these arguments. All the Justices had agreed on the *Sweatt* and *McLaurin* cases, so they knew what the attorneys for *Brown* would answer on the points the cases had in common. Is there evidence, asked Justice Stanley F. Reed, that black children's "ability to learn" is impaired by segregation?[14] Yes, said Robert L. Carter, the fund's attorney. Was "there a great deal more to the education process, even in the elementary schools, than what you read in the books?" Justice Harold H. Burton wanted to know. "Yes, that is precisely the point," agreed Mr. Carter. Justice William O. Douglas spelled it out when he said that "education is different" from other forms of segregation. The *Sweatt* and *McLaurin* decisions had gone beyond equal physical facilities to show that "things we cannot name are more

Thurgood Marshall, senior counsel of the NAACP Legal and Educational Defense Fund, who directed the case for the plaintiffs in *Brown* v. *Board of Education.*

important" to the students and cannot be found in segregated schools.[15]

Paul E. Wilson, counsel for the state of Kansas, expressed alarm that overruling *Plessy* meant telling some twenty states that they had been wrong in basing segregation laws on that case for so long. But Justice Burton didn't flinch from that conclusion.[16] Today's state law makers and courts, he pointed out, were operating under different social and economic conditions from those of the South seventy-five years before, when the Jim Crow laws had been adopted. Only Justice Felix Frankfurter sounded alarmed. The twenty states practicing segregation extended to the North. Was it really the job of the Court to reverse such a long-established practice, and to rule against every example of "man's inhumanity to man?"[17]

Thurgood Marshall commented on the South Carolina case of *Briggs* v. *Elliot*. Psychologists at the trial had shown that segregation destroyed a black child's self-respect. It "stamped him with a badge of inferiority."[18] Could the Supreme Court approve of the way the state court had ignored these mental injuries as a result of segregation? Justice Frankfurter said he could not accept such theories that he called "natural law," as grounds for making a sharp break with history, and declaring that segregation "is bad."[19] Marshall offered a more traditional argument. If a state distinguished in its laws between black and white citizens, it had to have a "reasonable" purpose—not just to give special privileges to whites. "I follow you," Justice Frankfurter told Marshall, "when you talk that way."[20]

After the first round of oral argument in December 1952, it was clear that for the Court the issue was greater than simply accepting the logic of the plaintiffs. The Justices might agree that a caste system, which put black citizens permanently on a lower level of society, was contrary to American principles and must be abolished. But there were two remaining problems: how to find an airtight legal basis for such a decision, which all nine Justices could support and which would persuade the opponents of school integration, and how to have the decision carried out.

Up to this point, the Court had been headed by Chief Justice Fred M. Vinson, who had written the *McLaurin* and *Sweatt* decisions but who hesitated to push for a nationwide order to desegregate all public schools. At the first conference of the Justices on the *Brown* case in December of 1952, Vinson seemed to be set on not reversing the *Plessy* formula of "separate but equal."[21] The Court postponed a decision, ordering lawyers on both sides of the *Brown* case to comb the historical record in order to find out what the framers of the Fourteenth

Amendment had meant to do about this question. Then, in the summer of 1953, Justice Vinson died suddenly, and President Dwight Eisenhower appointed Earl Warren, who had long been governor of California, to succeed him. In his many years as governor, Chief Justice Warren had developed the political skills to bring opposing sides together. He realized at once that *Plessy* would have to be reversed—black children could not in good conscience be sent any longer to inferior schools.[22]

But he also knew that he would need a good deal of time and patience to convince the other Justices to support that conclusion.

In the meantime, the NAACP attorneys worked day and night, with the help of many historians, to make it appear that integration of schools was in keeping with the thinking behind the Fourteenth Amendment. It was a discouraging task. The historical evidence was sketchy, since public schools had not played a major role in the America of the 1860s. But even without conclusive evidence, Marshall thought he could win on other points. Even a "nothing to nothing score" on what type of education the authors of the Fourteenth Amendment had in mind for black children, he told his associates, "means we win the ball game."[23]

The NAACP lawyers would have to persuade the Justices that education had become a much more central part of American life than it had been a century earlier. Further, they would need to have the Court accept that in the United States racism could no longer be allowed to be part of public education. Finally, when it came to proposing a remedy, how to fix the wrong done to black children in separate schools, the attorneys had to convince the Court that it had no choice. Once it ruled in favor of Linda Brown and the dozens of other plaintiffs, the Justices must order the end of segregation at once. At the very most, the lawyers concluded, the defendants might be given a year to make all the necessary changes and integrate the schools.[24] But to delay any longer would forever damage those children and deny them their constitutional rights.

4

The Case for the Board of Education

The black school children seeking a place in all-white schools were represented by the lawyers of the NAACP. More than twenty lawyers, under the guidance of Thurgood Marshall, had been working on the written and oral arguments made to the Supreme Court. There was no such central direction on the opposing side.

Each of the four states—Kansas, Delaware, Virginia, and South Carolina—that had segregated public schools sent its chief law officer, usually called the attorney general, to defend it. The fifth case to be included under the *Brown* v. *Board of Education* label was from the District of Columbia. Its chief lawyer was known as the corporation counsel. So, there were five different ideas on what defense strategy to follow.

For example, there had been a new election to the school board of Topeka, Kansas, which had denied Linda Brown admission to the Sumner School. The new board had begun to allow black children to enter white schools, so it did not want to defend the exclusion of Linda and other black children.[1] The Supreme Court ordered the Kansas attorney general to enter the case. He sent his assistant, Paul E. Wilson, to argue that, while the state did not favor the policy of segregation, it stood by its right to let its cities decide for themselves.[2]

The two southern states in the case, South Carolina and Virginia, were not as reluctant as Kansas to join the battle. They defended segregation as good public policy. If there was to be a senior spokesman for segregation, it would clearly be John W. Davis, a nationally known lawyer, who had been asked by South Carolina's governor, Jimmy Byrnes, to take the case. At that time, aged 79, Davis had argued 140 cases before the Supreme Court, more than anyone else.[3] As a law student, Thurgood Marshall had sometimes cut class to sit in on Davis's presentations at the Supreme Court. Davis had served in turn as a congressman from West Virginia, the United States government's solicitor general (top attorney), under President Woodrow Wilson, and ambassador to Great Britain; he had run as Democratic candidate for president in 1924, and for thirty years had been head of a very big Wall Street law firm.

A biography of Davis entitled *Lawyer's Lawyer* shows that he was held in high esteem by his colleagues.[4] Its author calls Davis "a man of gentle wit and superior learning," who "charmed almost everyone that he met."[5] Richard Kluger, author of *Simple Justice,* the classic account of the school integration cases, finds Davis full of "racial prejudices" and "at worst a closet white-supremacist," that is to say, someone who privately believed blacks were inferior human beings.[6] After reading Davis's briefs and oral arguments to the Supreme Court, it would seem that he was not at all impressed by the NAACP case. He may have underestimated the persuasive force of Thurgood Marshall. Whatever the correct view of Davis, there is little doubt of his commitment to his clients. He took no pay from South Carolina for his services, accepting only a silver tea service from the grateful state legislature.

For Davis, the argument for segregated schools was simple. According to historical record, the Fourteenth Amendment had not been intended to force public schools to be integrated. And the decisions of the Supreme Court, particularly *Plessy* v. *Ferguson,* settled the matter for all time. There comes a time, Davis said, when such a principle "has been so often announced, so confidently relied upon, so long continued, that it passes the limits of judicial discretion and disturbance."[7] The legal principle of following the rule of an earlier case, or precedent is called *stare decisis,* or "let the decision stand" from the Latin. Of course, such a principle gives the legal system stability, but it would never permit a major change in the thinking of the Court reflecting a changed society.

The Justices must have recognized that not only had the country changed from the days after the Civil War, but there had also been a major shift in the part that black citizens played in its life. Once they had largely been living in the South, working as farmers or in menial occupations such as waiters, porters, and domestic servants; then the most talented ones had moved north.[8] In the big cities they had found better jobs, decent housing, and a voice in government. New leaders had arisen to inspire black citizens not to settle for an inferior life under the pretense that it was equal to that led by whites.

Justice Burton asked Davis whether relations between the two races might have changed so much that old segregation laws were no longer constitutional.[9] Davis was ready with his reply: "Changed conditions cannot broaden the terminology of the Constitution."[10] For him this meant that individual states, not the national government, decided how to educate children, under their so-called police power. That power had been defined by the Court as the right to "prescribe regulations to promote the health, peace, morals, education, and good order of the people."[11] Since education had not been mentioned in the body of the Constitution, Davis also understood it to be among those powers either "reserved to the States . . . or to the people," according to the Tenth Amendment.

So, Davis was making what is known as a "states' rights" argument. It echoed the position of the southern states before the Civil War—denying the national government the right to limit the spread of slavery. Milton Korman, corporation counsel for the District of Columbia, even quoted from the infamous *Dred Scott* decision. Here the Court, in 1857, had said that Congress was wrong in prohibiting slavery in Missouri because that interfered with private property rights.[12] At least some of the Justices in 1952 must have been shocked to hear *Dred Scott* quoted as being applicable to current issues—as if the Civil War had not laid that issue to rest, or as if the Thirteenth, Fourteenth, and Fifteenth Amendments had not assured freed blacks of their full civil rights.

Davis tried to soften the states' rights argument by

putting it into a context of what was better for the children. Under the federal system, he asserted, local self-government could more easily determine the wishes of parents than national government as to what education suited their children best. Surely, he concluded, the Supreme Court did not want to sit as "a glorified Board of Education for the state of South Carolina."[13]

In rebuttal, Thurgood Marshall argued that "this Court," not state or even national legislatures, was the right place to define the "individual rights of the minority people."[14] Lawmakers decided by the wishes of the majority, so they would tend not to be receptive to the basic rights of those in the minority. After all, said Marshall, that was the logic the Court had followed in the recent cases where black graduate students had sought equal protection.[15]

What did the southern states think about the *Sweatt* and *McLaurin* decisions of 1950, which seemed to undermine the "separate but equal" rule? For Davis, they didn't matter because they did not specifically overturn *Plessy.* They simply extended the need for exact equality in the education of whites and blacks.[16] Here it must have been clear to the Justices that Davis was ignoring the fact that, even when all physical details of graduate schools were the same for black and white students, the

Court had found "intangible" factors, such as the prestige of the white school or the low morale of the segregated black students, to be the crucial arguments against continued segregation. Following those 1950 decisions affecting Texas and Oklahoma, other border states, including Kentucky, Arkansas, and West Virginia, had integrated their graduate schools without a legal contest.[17]

Why wouldn't it be just as simple for the Court to issue an order to integrate all public schools and to have everyone fall into line? Paul Wilson, arguing for Kansas, had answered, "In perfect candor, I must say to the Court that the consequences would probably not be serious."[18] There would only need to be a transition period in order to absorb black teachers and administrators into the school system. But for John Davis, arguing for South Carolina, integrating education would lead to dire consequences. Good fences make good neighbors, so Davis implied that from having schools in common it would only be a short step to marriage between whites and blacks, so-called miscegenation.[19] And he denied that his answer amounted to racism.

Far from it, Davis said. South Carolina had tried to have mixed schools under the carpetbaggers, during the Reconstruction period from 1865 to 1877, with terribly destructive results.[20] Even W. E. B. Du Bois had written against putting black children into white schools "where they are not wanted."[21] There were social scientists, Davis claimed, who didn't agree with the experts cited by the plaintiffs—and they thought that forcing children to be together would be bad for them. But Davis was using old history to apply to a new situation, and he was quoting Du Bois out of context.

Davis had no trouble finding quotations from Du Bois in favor of strengthening the black community, but Du Bois felt that way because of anger at the segregation of his own day. Given his lifelong struggle to open up opportunities for black people, Du Bois surely would have applauded allowing them to enter public schools. And Davis must have known that no one intended to "force" black children into white schools. Rather, they would be given a choice to enroll in decent schools instead of the run-down one-room schoolhouses many of them had been attending in the South. As for experts on his side, Davis had no one to match the parade of psychologists and educators the Legal Defense Fund had put on the witness stand.

At the original trial of *Briggs* v. *Elliot,* the Clarendon County, South Carolina, school board had invited expert testimony from E. R. Crow, superintendent of schools at Fort Sumter. Crow claimed to have heard from "Negro school administrators" who would "prefer to have schools of their own race."[22] Under cross-examination by Thurgood Marshall, however, Crow wasn't able to recall the names of these sources. Nor could he find evidence for his prediction that "the public schools of the state would be abandoned," if the courts ordered them to be integrated.[23] Such a biased witness lacked the standing of Dr. Kenneth Clark, the psychology professor from City College of New York, who had found black children in Clarendon County revealed "negative effects" and confused concepts of self-esteem as the victims of segregation.[24]

In the original *Brown* trial in Kansas, the NAACP expert had been Dr. Hugh Speer, an education professor at the small campus of the University of Kansas City. He had been asked if black children wouldn't be upset to be outnumbered fifty to one by whites in an integrated school. Dr. Speer was sure that they would be fine, based on the experience of ten black students in an elementary school of 210 children near his campus.

They were all "very happy, well adjusted, and they are there voluntarily."[25] It was just like jumping into the water for the first time, said Speer: kids adapted quickly. In the formerly white schools, a black child would "have the opportunity to learn to live with, to work with, to cooperate with, white children who are representative of approximately 90 percent of the population of the society in which he is to live."[26]

When he argued for the defense before the Supreme Court, Davis knew this record—and that, as Thurgood Marshall rebutted, not a single scientist had been found to contradict that "segregation harms the child."[27] Yet Davis tried to pick apart the evidence of damage caused by segregated schools in South Carolina. First, he said that Dr. Clark was the only expert for the plaintiffs to have visited the schools at Scott's Branch. That wasn't true, since Dr. Matthew Whitehead, an education professor from Howard University, had also testified. Dr. Whitehead had noticed many black children absent from school because they "were in the fields plowing and working"; that is, the truancy law was not being enforced to make blacks attend school.[28]

Then Davis minimized Dr. Clark's findings. An even greater percentage of black children in the North appeared to have a "confused self-image" than those in the South, Davis said, as shown by their preferring a white doll over a black one when they were asked to choose by Dr. Clark.[29] This result meant that the South Carolina schools were not to blame. But, contrary to Davis's conclusion, it could also mean that different forms of segregation in the North and South had equally harmful effects. It didn't take southern schools off the

Jefferson Thomas, a student at Central High School in Little Rock, Arkansas, being jeered at by a white crowd, while waiting for the bus home in September of 1957.

hook. It just put them in the larger picture of a society that was stacked, in school and out, against black citizens being filled with pride in who they were.

The lawyer for the District of Columbia, Milton Korman, also argued that black children were happier in their separate schools, which provided "a receptive atmosphere."[30] Their own "colored teachers" were able to impart "colored folklore," an essential part of their culture, according to Korman.[31] In integrated schools they were sure to meet with racial hostility. Korman's argument seems paternalistic, that is, to put down black children as simple-minded, to be taught folklore instead of science, and fragile, unable to deal with anger from white classmates.

"I got the feeling yesterday," said Thurgood Marshall in his final rebuttal, "that when you put a white child in a school with a whole lot of colored children, the child would fall apart or something. Everybody knows that is not true. Those same kids in Virginia and South Carolina—and I have seen them do it—they play in the streets together, they play on their farms together, they go down the road together, they separate to go to school, they come out of school and play ball together. They have to be separated in school."[32]

But for John Davis, it was those separate schools that were the foundation for racial peace in the South. For the

Supreme Court to order them to be integrated would cause turmoil and confusion. It would be contrary to what courts had been saying for a long time.

Davis rested his case on the decision of the South Carolina court in *Briggs* v. *Elliot*.

> When seventeen states and the Congress of the United States have for more than three-quarters of a century required segregation of the races in the public schools, and when this has received the approval of the leading appellate courts of the country including the unanimous approval of the Supreme Court of the United States . . . it is a late day to say such segregation is violative of fundamental constitutional rights. It is hardly reasonable to suppose that legislative bodies over so wide a territory . . . and great judges of high courts have knowingly defied the Constitution for so long a period, or that they have acted in ignorance of the meaning of its provisions. The constitutional principle is the same now that it has been throughout this period.[33]

The plaintiffs had painted for the Court a picture of injustice. Thousands of black children were waiting outside schools they were not permitted to enter, schools that were closer to home, better equipped and staffed than their present schools. Should they be told to wait again until newly built black schools would be ready, close in quality to white schools but still legally shut off from them? Why couldn't children be admitted to schools—avenues to a better life—without regard to their skin color?

The defense was painting a different picture of black and white children happily going their separate ways. The racial problems of the United States had been kept in check, thanks to the efforts of states and towns to keep the two sides apart yet remain fair to both. Could the judges restrain themselves from meddling and leave things as they were? Or would they be tempted to go beyond accepted constitutional truths to create a new right for black children that would cause turmoil in thousands of school districts?

The Supreme Court had among its nine members "liberals" inclined to side with the plaintiffs and "conservatives" sympathetic to the defense. Whether or not they would find common ground was in large part going to be determined by the man who presided over it—its new Chief Justice.

5

The Court Deliberates

The Supreme Court that Earl Warren came to head as Chief Justice in October 1953 was made up of eight men who had already been wrestling with the case of *Brown* v. *Board of Education* for ten months. Though these men in black robes called themselves "the Brethren," there hadn't been much brotherhood in their recent relations. For the past few years, under Chief Justice Frederick M. Vinson, the Justices had set a record for the number of dissents, opinions disagreeing with the majority of the Court, that they had written. Apart from their different ways of interpreting the laws, they also had personal dislikes and jealousies of each other that made even polite conversation among some of them difficult.[1]

One of the most notorious feuds on the Court

involved Justices Hugo L. Black, a leading liberal, and Robert H. Jackson, a leading conservative. In 1945, Jackson had asked Black to recuse himself, withdraw from sitting, on a case that involved pay for coal miners. (Each Justice must decide if he should withdraw from a particular case if he fears that a conflict of interest would not allow him to be impartial.) Black had decided not to withdraw even when he found out that the lawyer for the miners had been Black's law partner twenty years earlier. Jackson was especially upset, since he had expected to write the opinion of the majority in favor of the mine owners.[2] Now thanks to Black's vote, the Court's majority, five-to-four, swung to the side of the mine workers. Jackson wrote an angry dissent, opinion in disagreement.

The feud became public in 1946, when President Truman nominated the easy-going Vinson to be the new Chief Justice. While the Senate considered the nomination, Associate Justice Black headed the Court temporarily. At the time, Jackson was on leave, serving as chief prosecutor of the international court that was trying Nazi war criminals at Nuremberg, Germany. When Jackson held a news conference to deny that he had ambitions to be Chief Justice himself, he also revealed his feud with Black. This caused President Truman to exclaim, "The Supreme Court has really made a mess of itself."[3]

Truman expressed confidence that Vinson had the ability to bring together "opposing minds." Unfortunately, the one matter that a number of the Justices clearly agreed on was their lack of respect for Vinson's mind or legal training.[4]

When the Justices had first listened to the two sides of the *Brown* case in December 1952, it seemed highly unlikely that they would ever find common ground. On December 13, after they had read briefs and heard the first oral arguments, they held a crucial conference, which was chaired by Vinson. In that type of conference, the Chief Justice starts by reviewing the case. If the Justices had taken a preliminary vote on the case, the procedure would have been reversed, with the most junior member going first, so that recently appointed Justices would not be swayed by their seniors.

It was Justice Felix Frankfurter's later recollection that, had his colleagues gone on to vote at that first meeting, four of them—Vinson, Reed, Jackson, and Clark—would have upheld the case for segregated schools, while a bare majority, Frankfurter believed would not have agreed; there would have been "several opinions for the majority," and "that would have been catastrophic."[5] Frankfurter thought that in such a crucial

Justice Felix Frankfurter, shown here, helped to shape the *Brown* v. *Board of Education* decision.

case the country had to hear a united voice from the Court.

Justice William O. Douglas, a staunch liberal on the Court and a noted outdoorsman, later recalled that the lineup was even less favorable to school integration than Frankfurter remembered. In his autobiography, Douglas claimed that a vote in December 1952 would have gone five-to-four *in favor* of segregated schools.[6]

From Vinson's summary of the *Brown* case at their first conference, the other justices gathered that Vinson did not want to overturn the *Plessy* ruling calling for "separate but equal" schools.

Vinson was one of the "conservatives" on the Court, along with Stanley Reed, Robert H. Jackson, and Felix Frankfurter. This group of Justices tended to be wary of upsetting legal tradition, or of ruling against the powers of the government in order to expand the rights of the individuals.

Vinson had an additional reason for upholding a separate lifestyle for whites. He had grown up in a segregated society, as had Justices Black, in Alabama, Tom C. Clark, in Texas, and Stanley Reed, in Kentucky.

But being born in a particular part of the country did not automatically mean a Justice would react to the *Brown* case in any predictable fashion. Justice Hugo Black, for example, had grown up in rural Alabama and earned his law degree from the University of Alabama. He had even joined the Ku Klux Klan before he was elected to the U.S. Senate—news that created a national furor when President Franklin D. Roosevelt named him to the Supreme Court in 1937.[7] Yet Black had become the leading "liberal" on the Court. He was often in a minority of two with Justice Douglas in cases of free speech or the rights of defendants in a criminal trial. Black's commitment to the Bill of Rights—the first ten amendments to the Constitution—made him sympathetic to the claims of African Americans.

Justice Felix Frankfurter, the Court's intellectual star, seemed to have moved in the opposite direction, from liberal to conservative. Frankfurter was born in Vienna in 1882. He had come to the United States at the age of twelve. He learned English, attended City College of New York, and eventually graduated first in his class from Harvard Law School. He was a professor there for twenty-six years. He helped found the American Civil Liberties Union, to protect the right of free expression under the First Amendment.[8]

Frankfurter's heart clearly was on the side of black schoolchildren seeking the best possible education. His mind, however, kept raising legal objections. Frankfurter greatly respected the Supreme Court, and he feared that people would lose respect for it if it told them how to run their lives. Frankfurter's philosophy was called "judicial self-restraint." It meant that judges should leave to the people's elected representatives those crucial matters known as "political questions." Frankfurter also wanted judges to beware of writing their personal beliefs into law.[9] Congress rather than the courts should enact equal access to education. The Fourteenth Amendment had allowed for congressional action but none had been taken recently. Frankfurter's judicial caution put him at odds with "activist" Justice Douglas, the other former law professor on the Court.

Justice Robert Jackson, another leading conservative, had grown up in western New York and climbed the ladder of Democratic party politics. He had joined the Supreme Court in 1941. In the *Brown* case, Jackson was especially put off by the "sociological arguments" of Thurgood Marshall, which relied on demonstrating harm to black children who had been forced to attend segregated schools.[10] Justice Jackson may have been influenced by a memo written by William H. Rehnquist, then his law clerk and later himself a Chief Justice of the Court. Rehnquist's memo sharply disagreed with Marshall's argument that "a majority may not deprive a minority of its constitutional right." To the contrary, stated Rehnquist, "in the long run, it is the majority who will determine what the constitutional rights of the minority are."[11]

If Justice Jackson leaned toward the arguments of the southern states, Justice Stanley Reed—both a southerner and a conservative—was even more clearly on the side of segregated schools. Reed had been born in Kentucky, where he had attended private white schools. He graduated from Kentucky Wesleyan College and Yale University. As a Justice, Reed followed Frankfurter's belief in judicial self-restraint and a narrow view of civil liberties.

It was Justice Frankfurter who found a way to put off the decision to May 1953. He convinced his colleagues that they would all benefit from having the case reargued. Perhaps the NAACP lawyers could come up with a more satisfying answer to his questions asking for solid legal grounds against segregation.[12]

When May came around, however, there was a second round of stalling. This time Justice Frankfurter succeeded in keeping those still in favor of segregation from calling a vote. More questions were asked of Marshall and Davis: First, what was in the minds of the men who had adopted the Fourteenth Amendment regarding public schools? Second, what kind of order might the Court issue for integrating the schools—directing changes from Washington, or having

President Eisenhower poses with black leaders on June 23, 1958, following their conference on school integration. From Left to right: Lester B. Granger, Executive Secretary of the Urban League; Dr. Martin Luther King, Jr., President of the Southern Christian Leadership Conference; E. Frederic Morrow, administrative officer, White House; President Eisenhower; Roy Wilkins, Executive Secretary of the NAACP; William P. Rogers, Attorney General.

them supervised by federal courts in local districts? At the next round of argument scheduled for December 7, 1953, the Court also asked the United States Attorney General to present the government's position for the first time. Usually the Court asks the Solicitor General, but Attorney General Herbert Brownell Jr., decided to handle the matter himself.

Then, on September 3, 1953, Chief Justice Vinson died suddenly of a heart attack at age 63. Justice Frankfurter breathed a sigh of relief. "This is the first indication I have ever had," he said, "that there is a God."[13] Not only had Frankfurter shown little respect for Vinson's ability as a Chief Justice; he also seemed to have lost all hope that Vinson would be able to bring unity to the Court in the *Brown* case. The kind of division that had prevailed under Vinson undercut public respect for the Court—and, for Frankfurter, that seemed to have been an unforgivable failing.

Could Earl Warren do any better? President Eisenhower had told him that he was being appointed Chief Justice "because of my deep conviction that you are uniquely qualified."[14] Many observers knew, however, that Warren was not being picked for his legal qualifications as much as to pay off a political debt. During the 1952 Republican convention, Warren had thrown his California delegates to the side of Eisenhower.

They put him over the top in a close contest for the presidential nomination with Robert A. Taft. Eisenhower had agreed to name Warren to the first vacancy on the Supreme Court. On September 30, 1953, the president told his news conference, "to my mind [Warren] will make a great Chief Justice."[15] So, Warren became the first governor in United States history to be named directly to the Supreme Court.

Earl Warren himself pondered his limited legal experience: as a mediocre law student at the University of California—Berkeley, as district attorney of Alameda County, then as attorney general for the state of California. "All of this lack of experience weighed heavily on my mind as I thought about the fact that in a few hours I would be presiding over the highest Court in the land."[16]

Warren may not have had a brilliant legal record, but he did have a genius for leadership and an ability to appeal to citizens on different sides of an issue. This talent had earned him a record three terms as governor of California. Would he be able to make an appeal to the quarreling Justices to rise to the challenge of history? Might he yet succeed where Vinson had failed?

When he faced the southern Justices on the Court, Warren at once understood that a decision integrating public schools was especially hard to support for someone "born and reared in that part of the nation where segregation was a way of life and where everyone knew the great emotional opposition" that integration would arouse.[17] Warren pointed out how much easier it was for the nonsouthern members of the Court, knowing that they were not "in danger of being faced with animosity and harassment in our home states because of centuries-old patterns of life," to order black and white children to attend school together. In other words, even the Supreme Court of the United States is made up of human beings who worry how they'll get along with their neighbors.

It was not at all clear that Warren would even join the liberals on school integration. As California's attorney general during World War II, he headed a personal crusade to put Japanese Americans into refugee camps. Yet he remembered having gone to school with black classmates.[18] As governor, Warren was driven from place to place by a black chauffeur named Edgar Patterson. Years later, Patterson recalled the governor had asked him to tell what it was like growing up in the South—"and then I used to tell him about some of the things that happened in New Orleans, the way black kids felt."[19]

The group of men over whom Warren would preside were known for their many differences. Could he get them talking to each other, let alone seeing eye to eye in the key questions of the *Brown* case? Perhaps Warren's greatest asset was his ability to listen to each of his colleagues and to sense what they could support in common. As soon as he was appointed, he took three crucial steps. First, he got to know everyone in the court, from janitors to Justices; he found out what their interests were and about their families. He began by making friends with the Senior Justice, Hugo Black, letting him preside over conferences for several weeks until Warren could comfortably take over.[20]

Second, Warren's approach was marked by caution, like a poker player. Eisenhower had named him to a "recess appointment," which had to be reviewed by the Senate after it reconvened in January 1954. There the Judiciary Committee, headed by "Wild Bill" Langer, senator from North Dakota, held hearings at which a parade of witnesses cast slurs on Warren's character and patriotism. Langer had been annoyed that his suggested nominees for federal jobs had been passed over. Eisenhower rose to Warren's defense. The committee approved Warren's nomination by a twelve-to-three vote, which was confirmed by the full Senate without any dissenters on March 1, 1954.[21] Until that time, Warren was careful to avoid antagonizing southern senators by taking a public stand against segregated schools.

Third, when it came to the *Brown* case, Warren held frequent conferences, inviting all of the Justices to air their views. He was careful, however, not to ask them to vote, so they would not box themselves into clashing positions.[22] Warren was even more effective meeting the other Justices one-on-one, at lunch or some other informal setting. On those occasions he was a sympathetic listener, showing an appreciation of the southern roots or conservative leanings that troubled many a colleague. He agreed with the concern of some Justices that ordering southern schools to integrate would be a bombshell. It would have to be done diplomatically, with sufficient time to change a century-old system. At both the individual and group meetings, Warren would refrain from stating his own position—at least for some four months. By the time Earl Warren called for a conference at which the Justices were asked to vote, he could assume virtually everyone would drop his personal reservations and join the team that would become known in history—first sarcastically, then with respect—as "the Warren Court."[23]

6

The Decision

The Argument

Monday, December 7, 1953. The first day for the final round of oral argument in the case of *Brown* v. *Board of Education* had arrived. After years of arguing the cases in federal and state courts, the lawyers for the NAACP Legal Defense Fund had submitted hundreds of pages to the Supreme Court of the United States. Now they would once more come face to face with the nine Justices seated on a bench above them. The NAACP lawyers were prepared to argue against the case for segregated schools made by attorneys for the states of Kansas, Delaware, Virginia, and South Carolina, as well as the District of Columbia.

In the usual "oral argument," attorneys before the Supreme Court have a brief period in which to summarize their case, then a clerk turns on a desk light signaling that there are five minutes left. When a red light goes on, time is up—even if a lawyer is in midsentence. Any of the Justices can fire questions at the opposing attorneys at any time. The questions can be based on the record of the original trials or on the briefs, written arguments, that the Justices have had time to study. Within an hour or two, the court usually stops the proceedings and goes on to another case.

There were several unusual features in the *Brown* case: the dozens of plaintiffs (eight from Kansas, twenty from South Carolina, and many more from the other states and the District of Columbia), the number of defendants (four states, plus the District of Columbia), and the fact that the decision would have a national impact. After hearing the opening arguments a year before, the Supreme Court set aside another three entire days for oral argument. This time they wanted to know exactly what the men who drew up the Fourteenth Amendment had in mind about the segregated schools of their time.

The Justices of the Supreme Court asked the lawyers for both sides to comb the historical record for clues as to what they should do now. Nowhere else in the Constitution did there seem to be words that could provide the Justices with clear guidance. Only the first section of the Fourteenth Amendment declared that the individual states could not "deny to any person within [their] jurisdiction the equal protection of the laws." The lawyers had to explain whether those who wrote these words meant them to apply to education.

Spottswood W. Robinson III, a young black lawyer from Richmond, Virginia, was the first to speak for the NAACP. In a historical summary, he said that the "broad purpose" of the Fourteenth Amendment was to put an end to segregation and achieve equality in all fields, including education. Robinson quoted from the congressional debates in 1866, on the Fourteenth Amendment.[1] One congressman had specifically said that schools would be included.

Justice Felix Frankfurter then asked Robinson how important one congressman's comment was. The NAACP lawyer insisted that his reading of these debates proved that education was covered, since no one in Congress had said it was not. Justice Frankfurter was not satisfied that this argument was good enough.[2] The history of the Fourteenth Amendment did not give convincing proof that the Congressman had intended to include the right of black children to attend white schools among those rights that no state could deny.

Then it was the turn of Thurgood Marshall, the chief lawyer for the NAACP. He concentrated not on the past but on the present. Marshall argued that it was proper for the Supreme Court today, under the Fourteenth Amendment, to put an end to segregated schools. Justice Robert H. Jackson said he had serious doubts about the courts stepping in where Congress had failed to act.[3] Marshall answered that just because Congress had not clearly acted it was even more important for the Justices to interpret the Constitution. This ended the first round for the NAACP lawyers.

It was time for the segregated states to argue their case. John W. Davis, attorney for South Carolina, answered the NAACP lawyers. He said that those who wrote the Fourteenth Amendment "did not understand [intend] that it would abolish segregation in public schools." Indeed, the federal government had always permitted segregated schools to operate in the District of Columbia. The "equal protection" offered by the Fourteenth Amendment, Davis said, was never meant to lead to interracial, or mixed-race, schools.[4]

On Tuesday, December 8, 1953, the NAACP lawyers got another turn to make the case against segregated schools. Again, Thurgood Marshall spoke. He said that if the Court endorsed separate black schools it would be saying that "Negroes are inferior to all other human beings."[5] In Marshall's eloquent words, school segregation implied:

an inherent determination that the people who were formerly in slavery, regardless of anything else, shall be kept as near that stage as is possible, and now is the time, we submit, that this Court should make it clear that that is not what our Constitution stands for.[6]

The rest of the December 8 and 9 arguments were taken up by eight other attorneys, including the Assistant Attorney General of the United States, J. Lee Rankin. He had submitted written papers as *amicus curiae*, "a friend of the court." But the views of the Justice Department had not been clear, so Justice William O. Douglas asked what the government's position on segregated schools really was. Rankin answered, "It is the position of the Department of Justice that segregation in public schools cannot be maintained under the Fourteenth Amendment."[7] Rankin went on to argue that it was significant that the framers of the Fourteenth Amendment had never said that they intended to *preserve* school segregation. Their silence left the court free to strike down the provision of separate schools for black and white schoolchildren. This comment implied that the new President of the United States, Dwight D. Eisenhower, supported the integration of schools as had his predecessor, Harry S. Truman. The fact that Eisenhower was concerned about southern resistance to integration was reflected in Rankin's suggestion that at least a year would be required to come up with a plan to enforce such an order by the Court. Rankin agreed with Justice Jackson that integrating schools would have to be done "school district by school district," supervised by local judges.[8]

The Deliberation

Saturday morning, December 12, 1953. While the arguments were still fresh in their minds, the nine Justices assembled behind the closed doors of their conference room to discuss the five desegregation cases. Their custom was to begin with the Chief Justice, newly appointed Earl Warren. Each Justice would make a brief statement, in order of seniority, about how the case should be decided. After they had a chance to discuss issues they disagreed on, the Justices would vote in reverse order, beginning with Sherman Minton, the newest Associate Justice and ending with Earl Warren.

Earl Warren began by trying to persuade his colleagues that the old doctrine of "separate but equal" could not be upheld because it implied the inferiority of black people. Whatever might have been the intent of those who drafted the Fourteenth Amendment eighty-five years earlier, segregated schools could no longer be justified.

When the other Justices took their turn at expressing

Chief Justice Earl Warren, shown here, wrote the Supreme Court opinion in the *Brown* v. *Board of Education* case.

their opinions, it appeared there was a majority in agreement with Warren. But the Chief Justice needed more than a majority vote. He needed to impress the South with a unanimous judgement by the Supreme Court, with every Justice in agreement. So he suggested that the Justices put off a formal vote for a month or two and continue to think and to talk with each other.[9]

Over the next few weeks, Chief Justice Warren talked with each of the Associate Justices. He impressed on them how essential it was to write a unanimous decision in such a big case. By early March of 1954, Warren was able to persuade all of the Justices to agree that segregated schools were no longer constitutional. The last holdout for segregation was Justice Reed. Warren told him, "Stan, you're all by yourself in this now. You've got to decide whether it's really the best thing for the country."[10] Justice Jackson still wanted to write a separate but "concurring" opinion, to spell out his differences while agreeing with the majority. Then on March 30, 1954, he suffered a heart attack and needed several weeks to recover from it. Warren visited him in the hospital, leaving drafts of the opinion he had been writing, and with one minor change, Jackson went along.[11] To Warren's alarm, Justice Jackson even "insisted on dressing and coming to the Court for the announcement."[12]

The Decision

Monday, May 17, 1954. When the nine Justices took their seats, spectators in the courtroom had no idea that the school desegregation decision would be announced that day. It appeared to be a routine day. One hundred eighteen new lawyers were admitted to practice before the Supreme Court. Three minor opinions were read by Justice Tom Clark and Justice William O. Douglas. They concerned cases dealing with milk sales in Chicago, the collection of fines from a federal employee found guilty of negligence, and the picketing of retail stores by a bakery union.

Only then did Earl Warren begin, "I have for announcement the judgement and opinion of the Court in No. 1, *Brown et al.* v. *Board of Education of Topeka et al.*" (Et al. is from Latin, meaning "and others.")[13] Suddenly reporters who had been waiting in the press room downstairs followed the Court's press officer into the courtroom. In a firm, clear, and unemotional voice, the Chief Justice read his opinion to a hushed audience:

> We conclude that in the field of public education the doctrine of "separate but equal" has no place. Separate educational facilities are inherently unequal.[14]

With these words, the Supreme Court ended forever legally enforced segregation in public schools. *Plessy* v. *Ferguson*, the 1896 case, described in Chapter 2, that had judged "separate but equal" to be acceptable under the

Constitution, was no longer the law with respect to public schools.

The Opinion

When a court makes a decision, it often writes an opinion explaining how it reached its decision. The opinion must explain how the legal precedents, similar cases that have been decided before this one, apply to this case. The *Brown* decision had to do this, and more, because it had to justify the decision in language that ordinary citizens could understand.

Chief Justice Earl Warren wrote the decision, but all eight other Justices agreed with it. He explained that the Court could not just look at the language of the Fourteenth Amendment, for in 1866, those who wrote it didn't really think about what schools children would attend. There was no universal public education in 1868, when the amendment was accepted by the states. But the world of 1954 was completely different.

> In approaching this problem, we cannot turn the clock back to 1868 when the Amendment was adopted, or even to 1896 when *Plessy* v. *Ferguson* was written. We must consider public education in light of its full development and its present place in American life throughout the Nation.[15]

In the United States today, public schools are probably the most important business of local

The News

HIGH COURT BANS SEGREGATION IN PUBLIC SCHOOLS

On the steps of the Supreme Court in Washington, D.C., Mrs. Nettie Hunt explains the Court's decision ending school segregation to her daughter.

government. There are laws that require an education be provided for all children. Great amounts of money are spent on education, because we believe schooling to be essential to democracy.[16]

So the question the Justices asked was: "Does segregation deprive members of the minority race of equal educational opportunities?" The answer for all nine members of the court was, without a doubt, "Yes." They said that legally enforced segregation "generates a feeling of inferiority . . . that may affect . . . hearts and minds in a way unlikely to be undone."[17] This feeling of inferiority can affect the motivation of a child to learn, and slow down his or her mental and educational development. Such children would then not have an equal opportunity to succeed later in life.

That's why, the Supreme Court concluded, separate but equal has no place in America when it comes to education. The plaintiffs had been deprived of the equal protection of the laws, in violation of the Fourteenth Amendment.

The Court dealt separately with the District of Columbia case, *Bolling* v. *Sharpe*, because the Fourteenth Amendment applies only to state actions and this case came from the nation's capital which does not qualify as a state. But the national government must obey the Fifth Amendment, which guarantees that "no person shall be . . . deprived of life, liberty, or property, without due process of law."[18] The Supreme Court found that black school children were being denied the "liberty" to attend schools of their choice, without "due process," that is, unfairly. Since the Court had just made the states desegregate their schools, Chief Justice Warren said, "It would be unthinkable that the same Constitution would impose a lesser [responsibility] on the Federal Government."[19]

After nearly sixty years of approving legal segregation, the Supreme Court had found a way around the *Plessy* decision, and had taken the first step toward breaking down segregated public education.

When the Civil War had ended in 1865, white and black children were kept apart in much of the country. In 1954, about forty percent of *all* the students in the public schools of the United States still attended segregated schools—a total of 8,200,000 white children and 2,530,000 black children.[20] When Linda Carol Brown of Topeka, Kansas, the Pearson and Briggs children, of Clarendon County, South Carolina, and Spottswood Bolling, of Washington, D.C., won their day in the Supreme Court, so did all those millions of other children—and future generations to come.

What remained to be spelled out was how the Court's decision would be enforced. On that crucial point, the nine Justices could not yet agree—and they decided to put the matter off for another year.

7

The Impact of the Brown Decision

The entire country was in an uproar when it learned of the *Brown* decision. The news flashed instantly across radio and television programs. The next morning, May 18, 1954, banner headlines in newspapers announced, "High Court Bans School Segregation."[1] The decision was called "the most important [opinion] on racial relations since the Supreme Court ruled before the Civil War that Dred Scott, a Negro slave, was not a citizen."[2] Other stories told of southern resistance.

Governor Herman Talmadge of Georgia said the Court's decision had reduced the Constitution to "a mere scrap of paper."[3] Even respected members of Congress from the South called for defiance. Senator Richard B.

Russell, who headed the Southern Democratic Caucus, said, "Ways must be found to check the tendency of the Court to disregard the Constitution."[4] Senator Harry F. Byrd of Virginia saw the *Brown* decision as "the most serious blow that has yet been struck against the rights of the states."[5] Senator James O. Eastland of Mississippi vowed that the South "will not abide by nor obey this legislative decision by a political court. We will take whatever steps are necessary to retain segregation in education."[6]

At the Supreme Court, Chief Justice Warren had been able to bring about a unanimous Court by focusing on the injustice of forcing black children to attend separate schools. Some of the reluctant Justices would go along with Warren only because they would have another year to decide on a so-called decree, an order to make *Brown* the practice in thousands of school districts.

The May 1954 opinion became known to lawyers as *Brown I.* How it would be put into effect—a follow-up to the original decision—was a case called *Brown II,* which began later that year. Now, in the face of mounting southern protest, the NAACP lawyers again had to present briefs to the Court on a timetable to integrate schools. No matter how unpleasant it might be for southern whites, they argued, all schools should be opened to black children by the fall of 1955 and integration completed a year later.[7]

Attorneys for the southern states competed in submitting plans that would stretch our forever the date for integrating schools. They wanted the maximum freedom left to each school district, and they sketched in lurid colors how passionately white parents would resist the Court's order. In the last round of oral argument, in April 1955, Emory S. Rogers represented South Carolina instead of John W. Davis, who had died a few weeks before the hearings. Rogers managed to arouse the anger of the normally even-tempered Chief Justice.

> *Rogers:* I do not think . . . the white people of the district will send their children to the Negro schools . . . . But I do think that something can be worked out. We hope so.

> *Warren:* It is not a question of attitude; it is a question of conforming to the decree . . . . But you are not willing to say here that there would be an honest attempt to conform to this decree, if we did leave it to the district court [to implement]?

> *Rogers:* No, I am not. Let us get the word "honest" out of there.

> *Warren:* No, leave it in.

> *Rogers:* No, because I would have to tell you that right now we would not conform; we would not send our white children to the Negro schools.[8]

In the face of white southern resistance, Warren came

91

to share the moderate position of the U.S. Attorney General, Herbert Brownell Jr., who had been asked once again to submit the government's brief on this question. Brownell reflected the caution of his boss, President Eisenhower, in not pushing a rigid timetable upon the resisting southern school districts. Federal district courts should supervise the process of integration, Brownell said. They would know how much weight to give to local conditions. There would undoubtedly be "popular hostility," Brownell concluded, but that should not furnish a legal excuse "for a failure to end school segregation. Racial segregation in public schools is unconstitutional and will have to be terminated as quickly as feasible."[9]

When it came to the specific language that Warren would draft for his opinion, Justice Frankfurter hit upon a phrase used many years earlier by Justice Oliver Wendell Holmes: "With all deliberate speed."[10] This did not mean that district courts should go slowly in issuing their orders, but that the actual enrollment of black students, district by district, could be on a flexible schedule. Unfortunately, the phrase seemed to send a mixed message. The Supreme Court wanted southern whites to demonstrate "speed" in dismantling separate schools, but southerners would read "deliberate" as

The 1954 Supreme Court that decided the *Brown* v. *Board of Education* case. Front row, from left to right: Felix Frankfurter, Hugo L. Black, Earl Warren, Stanley Reed, William O. Douglas. Back row, from left to right: Tom C. Clark, Robert H. Jackson, Harold H. Burton, and Sherman Minton.

permitting them to argue about details almost indefinitely.

On April 16, 1955, the Court assembled for a final conference. Eight of the Justices were the same men who had been wrestling with the *Brown* case for nearly three years. But Justice Jackson had died the previous fall, and President Eisenhower named John Marshall Harlan to the ninth seat. Harlan was the grandson of the Justice of the same name who, in 1896, had written the stirring dissent to the *Plessy* decision, asserting that the Constitution should be "color-blind." The present Justice Harlan, however, soon joined the conservatives on the Court—those Justices who preferred a generally cautious to an activist approach by the courts.[11]

At the conference, all of the Justices, including Harlan, agreed that they had to maintain the unanimity of the opinion in the decree that would put it into force. The differences that they expressed were based on their estimate of how strongly the South would resist an order to desegregate. Justice Black spoke for the pessimists. As an Alabaman, he expected his fellow southerners not to obey the Court on this question for another generation. "It is futile to think," said Black, "that in these cases we can settle segregation in the South."[12] At best, a short, direct decree might get the process under way by ordering that the plaintiffs—the children whose parents had brought the suit—be admitted to the schools that had turned them away because of their skin color.

Justice Frankfurter spoke for the optimists, noting that during the past year border states such as Maryland, West Virginia, and Kentucky, had begun to open their schools to black children. He expected this example to spread to the South itself.[13] Justice Clark commented that there hadn't been "too much trouble in Texas," his native state.[14] Even Justice Reed, the last holdout in the original decision, thought that, in general, southerners would cooperate with the Court's order.

Chief Justice Earl Warren wrote the opinion in *Brown II*, and read the seven paragraphs to a packed courtroom on May 31, 1955. Warren's words sounded as if he wanted to meet halfway the critics who had been grumbling that the Supreme Court was setting itself up as a school board for the entire country. The opinion made clear that the "primary responsibility" for solving all the problems of integrating schools would rest on the "school authorities" in each district.[15] Federal district courts that would oversee the school boards were to be guided by "a practical flexibility," taking into account "different local conditions." The Supreme Court merely insisted that the defendants "make a prompt and reasonable start."

The opinion then went on to list the kinds of

problems that could convince local courts to give school boards extra time: the physical condition of school buildings, the transportation system, necessary adjustments in district lines, etc. The Court pointed out that it would not allow delay simply because school officials disagreed with the integration of schools. But in its final sentence, the Court appeared to leave southerners a loophole. It ordered the admission of black children "to public schools on a racially nondiscriminatory basis with all deliberate speed."[16] The last three words were taken by the defenders of racially separate schools as a signal that they could drag their heels. In dozens of southern districts, federal judges who lived there allowed school officials to stall year after year. Ten years later, only 1 percent of black youngsters in the South were attending school with whites.

Some of the eleven southern states were openly defiant about obeying the Supreme Court. In Mississippi, Governor Hugh L. White declared, "We're not going to pay any attention to the Supreme Court decision. We don't think it will have any effect on us down here at all."[17] In South Carolina, Governor Jimmy Byrnes (who had served for a year on the United States Supreme Court) expressed "supreme confidence that we will find ways to lawfully maintain segregation."[18] Even Governor Orval Faubus of Arkansas, who had been moderate on racial issues, found that taking an extremist stand against integrated schools seemed likely to assure him a third term in office.

A federal district court had accepted a plan by the school board of Little Rock, Arkansas, to integrate public schools over several years, beginning in 1957. When nine black students showed up at Central High School on September 3 of that year, however, they found the school had been put "off limits" by the governor.[19] He had ordered National Guard troops to surround the empty school, to defend it against a "mob" that hadn't shown up. The district court ordered the school board to go ahead with integration, no matter whether there might be protests. Yet, the next morning—and for three more weeks—the guardsmen standing shoulder to shoulder blocked entrance to the black children who tried to attend school each day. On September 23, the black students succeeded in entering the school, as the federal judge had ordered, but three hours later, the police made them go home. Now there really was a white mob outside.

Up to this point, President Eisenhower had been careful not to express his own opinion on the *Brown* decision. He merely said that, as the chief executive, he had to enforce the Constitution as interpreted by the Supreme Court. Now the president could not let the governor openly defy the law. He ordered a fleet of Army trucks and jeeps carrying a thousand paratroopers to drive up to Little Rock the night of September 24. He also "federalized" the National Guard. That is, he put the state troops under the United States Army command. The next morning, the nine black students entered Central High School under military escort. For the rest of the school year these children suffered all kinds of abuse from gangs of segregationists, who kicked them, spat on them, and even poured soup on one of them in the cafeteria.[20]

In February 1958, the city school board asked the federal court to delay integration for another two and a half years, in view of the "chaos, bedlam, and turmoil" the local police would not be able to control once the federal troops were gone.[21] The trial court granted the request, but a federal appeals court overruled it. The United States Supreme Court scheduled a special session to deal with this case before the 1958 school year began. Chief Justice Warren spoke for a unanimous court in the case known as *Cooper* v. *Aaron*. Neither violence nor the threat of violence, he wrote, could be used as an excuse for delaying school desegregation. As Justice Frankfurter added in a concurring opinion, "Violent resistance to law cannot be made a reason for its suspension."[22]

There was national sympathy for the courageous

black children in Little Rock who had to pass jeering mobs daily in order to attend school. The violence there—and in New Orleans, in Oxford, Mississippi, and in Clinton, Tennessee—was dramatic, but violence was far from the only obstacle to the enrollment of black children. Hundreds of other school districts successfully used "red-tape" regulations to prevent their enrollment.[23] So-called "pupil placement laws" in North Carolina, Alabama, and other states allowed indefinite delays in admitting black students until school boards had examined their academic and physical condition, morals, conduct, etc. But in such cases that slowed integration to a snail's pace into the 1960s, the Supreme Court did not find in favor of the black children.[24] The justices seemed satisfied that a tiny handful of black students had achieved being admitted to previously all-white schools, even though most of the original plaintiffs—except those in Washington, D.C.—never managed to enjoy the "equal protection of the laws" to which the Court had said they were entitled.[25] There was only one case of defiance so flagrant that the Court felt compelled to speak out.

The original *Brown* case had included black plaintiffs from Prince Edward County, Virginia, who had been turned away from white schools there in 1951. In 1964, thirteen years later, not a single black child had been admitted. Over the previous four years, the county had closed all of its public schools rather than desegregate them. The state of Virginia had passed a law funding private schools, which were attended by white children in the county, but not by blacks, who kept asking the courts to reopen the public schools. The Supreme Court, in an opinion written by Justice Black, found that in this case "there has been entirely too much deliberation and not enough speed in enforcing the constitutional rights" affirmed in 1954.[26] The federal district court was empowered to end the state grants of tuition and tax credits to the parents of white children in private schools, although Justices Clark and Harlan dissented from the majority opinion that the Court should order the public schools reopened.

Why did the Court wait until 1964 to show its impatience with the failure of nearly all southern districts to follow *Brown* and open public schools to all, regardless of race? To some degree, the changed mood of the Justices reflected a different feeling in the White House, the Congress, and the country. President Eisenhower had been succeeded in 1960 by John F. Kennedy, then in 1963 by Lyndon B. Johnson. The Eisenhower attitude of caution toward stirring up resistance to integration in the South had given way to Kennedy's and Johnson's open commitment to civil rights.[27] Congress had responded in

1964 by passing the strongest Civil Rights Act since the Civil War. This law not only abolished discrimination in restaurants, motels, gas stations, theaters, sports arenas, and other "public accommodations"; it also had the United States Office of Education draw up guidelines for desegregating schools, and it authorized the Justice Department to bring suit "for the orderly achievement of desegregation in public education."[28]

Perhaps the most effective new weapon of the 1964 Act was the power given to the Department of Health, Education, and Welfare to cut off federal funds from school districts that didn't integrate their schools. Feeling the economic pressure from Washington, more and more southern school officials admitted black children to formerly all-white schools. By the late 1960s, a few outspoken judges in federal district courts put an end to "tokenism" and so-called freedom of choice plans, which had allowed white children to opt out of integrated schools. In key decisions, courts adopted numerical measures as a standard of integration—ruling against both the exclusion of black school children from white schools and the failure of school districts to find new jobs for black teachers in formerly all-black schools.[29]

The changed feeling in the country by the mid-1960s was due largely to a shift in tactics by black activists. No longer were they content to send lawyers to assert claims for equality in the nation's court in cases that dragged on for years. Instead, blacks used mass protests and "nonviolent resistance" to claim their rights—to vote in the Deep South, to be served at lunch counters, and to attend decent schools. Young people joined militant organizations, such as the Congress of Racial Equality (CORE) and the Student Nonviolent Coordinating Committee (SNCC), that made "black power" their goal. The NAACP's platform of integration seemed to be losing some of its relevance. And the activists who had filed lawsuits were harassed and physically attacked throughout the South.[30]

Had the battle for integrated schools been worth it? Howard University professor Alois Adair and other black scholars doubted it. They claimed that even in desegregated schools there was no lessening of white control.[31] And most black schoolchildren, whether attending schools with or without white classmates, were still to be found in run-down buildings and receiving an inferior education. Wealthier whites, especially in the North, had moved to the suburbs, where their children enjoyed the best schooling that their tax money could buy. In 1968, black parents in Texas challenged the system of financing schools out of property taxes, which kept poor children in poor schools. In 1973, the Supreme Court, by a five-to-four vote, upheld unequal schools when these were due to differences between rich and poor neighborhoods. The majority seemed to reject Chief Justice Warren's claim in 1954 that education "is the very foundation of good citizenship"—instead, it now denied that education is "among the rights afforded explicit protection under our Federal Constitution."[32]

Has the *Brown* decision, then, turned into a failure? There is no easy answer, because the original racial issue has become clouded by economic factors. For urban blacks living in the "ghettos" of decaying cities, both North and South, schools have not assured a way out to a better life. For a new class of black professionals, however, it has been possible to secure a good education for their children, and for those with college degrees to close the gap between their incomes and those of whites. Perhaps those who supported integration in *Brown* had overestimated the immediate benefits of their legal victory. But by 1972, nearly half of southern black children were attending integrated schools—and enjoying a feeling of equal rights. These equal rights extended past educational opportunity into running for and winning political office, using public facilities, and obtaining a decent standard of living.[33]

Ironically, the struggle for equality has been relatively harder for blacks in the North, who have encountered more inflexible housing segregation than their southern counterparts. And in the area of equalizing schooling, federal judges have turned increasingly to busing as a solution. The first major use of court-ordered busing in the South, in Charlotte, North Carolina, had succeeded in overcoming white resistance in 1971.[34] But a federal order to bus children in Boston, to achieve racial balance, led to a major explosion in 1974. By 1976, some twenty thousand white students had left the public schools for private or Catholic school education. In Boston's public schools, black students were now in the majority. And their parents were expressing uncertainty that it had been worth it to subject their children to the harassment.[35]

In 1972, an even more ambitious program than the one in Boston brought busing to the schools of Detroit, another northern city that had experienced "white flight" to the suburbs. Federal Judge Stephen Roth's order linked the predominantly black city schools with fifty-three white suburban school systems—a total of three hundred thousand children. But Michigan Governor William Milliken lodged a legal challenge that reached the Supreme Court in 1974. A new Chief Justice, Warren Burger, had succeeded Earl Warren in 1969, and he led a five-man majority in overturning the busing decree. His logic: the suburbs had not caused Detroit's segregation and, therefore, they need not help to solve the problem.[36] Thurgood Marshall, who had joined the court in 1967, sadly said in his dissent that the Court was now turning back the clock, responding "to a perceived public mood that we have gone far enough in enforcing the Constitution's guarantee of equal justice."[37]

The Burger opinion in the Detroit case, *Milliken* v. *Bradley* did indeed mark a step backward from the standards of *Brown* v. *Board of Education.* It erected a new hurdle for black plaintiffs: they had to identify someone responsible for a denial of their rights before they could claim their equality as United States citizens. The Court, which had been willing twenty years before to pull down the walls of white privilege in the South, was not ready to break the walls of exclusion in the northern suburbs.

Nathan Glazer, a Harvard University professor of education recognized that busing had had disappointing results in achieving integration. Yet Dr. Glazer asserted that "true integration" was a worthwhile goal in education, because it would permit children "of various ethnic and racial backgrounds [to] meet with each other and know each other."[38] Only as the promise of *Brown* was realized, and black children were not refused admission to any school on account of their race, he argued—would we be able to create "an integrated society in the U.S." Already we could appreciate the fruits of *Brown:* the thousands of blacks in northern and southern colleges; the black professionals and employees working in government, the universities, and businesses; the steady rise in black incomes; the millions of black voters who had been electing members of school boards, state legislatures, and Congress.

The Courts had helped to open the doors to schools. The judges could show the way to a system of educational opportunity that would be equal for all. Yet even today this goal has not been fully achieved. One reason might be that people in positions of privilege, by virtue of their wealth and other advantages, believed that they would have to make some sacrifices first, that is, they would have to give up something for the common good.

There is no doubt in the mind of Columbia University professor of education, Diane Ravitch, that better schools do make a difference—that they have "produced measurable gains for disadvantaged children."[39] In her opinion, the *Brown* decision was a crucial step on the road to black progress, but many other steps still have to be taken before the United States attains true equality for *all* of its citizens.

Questions to Think About

1. It may be hard to imagine arguments, common some forty years ago, that black children should be kept out of public schools just because that had been done for a long time. Yet the states that defended separate schools for blacks and whites didn't only rely on "precedent." What do you think of the other questions they raised? Why not let each state, with its unique problems, have the freedom to work these out? What is the danger if the Supreme Court sets itself up as a "national board of education," depriving local school boards of the opportunity to work on plans for change?

2. Much of Linda Brown's case rested on the findings of psychologists who said that black children in segregated schools developed a poor self-image. How could you back up such an argument when challenged by the defense that such tests reveal poor self-images even when children attend integrated schools in the North? Also, are such test results permanent or could they change from time to time? If they were changeable, how would it affect this argument that schools should be desegregated?

3. How would Thurgood Marshall (for the plaintiffs) counter defense arguments that separate schools for black children may help, rather than hurt, their progress—given that Marshall himself was a product of segregated public schools, a black college, and a black law school? Is there merit in the plaintiffs' arguments that segregated schools are bad, because (a) they *forcibly* keep black children out of all-white schools, (b) schools for black children generally get less public funding, and (c) a segregated education might impair the self-confidence of many, if not all, black students?

4. Look up the newspaper files in your library that announced the *Brown* v. *Board of Education* decision on May 18, 1954. What were the key points that were highlighted in the news stories and editorials? Did the

way the decision was presented—by a unanimous Court, in brief, simple language—make it more dramatic? What problems in enforcing the decision did the news accounts foresee? How do you think schools in your area were affected?

5. Were the Justices of the Supreme Court too optimistic about the readiness of the South to accept an order to integrate schools? Was it better to wait a year for an enforcement order, or should such an order have been part of the original decision? What might the Court have done to avoid the resistance and delay by southern governors and other officials? Was it fair to have the Court tell Linda Brown and other black children that they had a legal right to attend school regardless of their skin color? Was it fair to make them wait such a long time for this to take effect?

6. Within twenty years of the *Brown* decision, black citizens had joined a movement for "black power." How does school integration appear in this new perspective—which puts top priority on the need for black citizens to control their own communities—rather than be admitted to a society run by whites? How would you encourage separate black schools and colleges, as essential for learning about black history and culture? Is

there any remedy for the hundreds of black teachers and school administrators who lost their jobs when their all-black schools closed?

7. It could be said that schools haven't really changed all that much since 1954. Many of them, especially in our central cities, are still attended largely by children of minority groups, while white children go to schools in the suburbs. Does this new form of segregated education deprive both white and black children of crucial learning experiences? What are reasons for and against having judges order children to be bused to create a "balanced" school population? How would it be possible to redraw school district lines so that city and suburban schools are linked, and children can attend schools according to their performance?

8. The 1964 Civil Rights Act seems to have opened up formerly segregated restaurants, parks, swimming pools, motels, and other facilities, without any major opposition. Why has it been so much harder to have parents accept the need for their children to attend school regardless of race? Have open schools helped to open other opportunities for blacks? To what extent has the guarantee of black voting rights and the presence of

black officials, locally and nationally, helped the United States to achieve a multicultural society?

9. Many social scientists have criticized the gap in incomes in the United States between black and white families, and the relatively greater proportion of blacks who are still trapped in poverty. How can an integrated, and better-quality education help black students to rise on the economic scale? Why do you think segregated schools tend to have high dropout rates?

10. Perhaps the self-images and prejudices of children are already set by the time they enroll in first grade. How would a preschool program, such as Head Start, help to improve their progress? In what other ways could local or national programs back up the contribution of integrated schools? Are there ways to overcome segregated housing patterns? What are some advantages and disadvantages of the present system of financing public schools mainly through property taxes?

Chapter Notes

Chapter 1

1. Daniel M. Berman, *It Is So Ordered: The Supreme Court Rules on School Desegregation*, New York: W.W. Norton, 1966, p. 9.

2. *Kansas City Star*, May 17, 1964. Interview with Mrs. Brown, cited in John D. Weaver, *Warren: The Man, the Court, the Era*, Boston: Little, Brown, 1967, p. 211.

3. United States Supreme Court, *Transcript of Oral Arguments, No. 8, Brown v. Board of Education*, 1952, pp. 89–90.

4. *Ibid.*, p. 90.

5. *Ibid.*, pp. 91–92.

6. Richard Kluger, *Simple Justice: The History of Brown v. Board of Education and Black America's Struggle for Equality*, New York: Knopf, 1987, p. 409.

7. United States Supreme Court, *Transcript of Oral Arguments, No. 101, Briggs v. Elliot*, 1952, p. 94.

8. *Ibid.*, p. 7.

9. *Ibid.*, pp. 52–55.

10. *Ibid.*, p. 59–60.

11. *Ibid.*, pp. 40–41.

12. Kluger, p. 18.

13. *Ibid.*, p. 23.

14. *Ibid.*

15. *Ibid.*, p. 24.

16. United States Supreme Court, *Transcript of Oral Arguments, No. 101, Briggs v. Elliot*, 1952, pp. 84–89.

17. *Ibid.*, p. 275.

18. *Ibid.*, p. 189.

19. *Ibid.*, p. 208.

20. United States Supreme Court, *Transcript of Oral Arguments, No. 413, Bolling v. Sharpe*, 1952, pp. 4–5.

21. Lee Arbeitman and Richard L. Roe, *Great Trials in American History*, St. Paul, MN: West Publishing Co., 1985, p. 85.

22. Kluger, p. 518.

23. United States Supreme Court, *Transcript of Oral Arguments, No. 413, Bolling v. Sharpe*, 1952, pp. 37–41.

24. *Ibid.*, pp. 37–41.

25. *Ibid.*

26. *Bolling v. Sharpe*, 347 U.S. 497.

27. Kluger, p. 523.

Chapter 2

1. Rhoda L. Blumberg, *Civil Rights: The 1960s Struggle*, Boston: Twayne, 1991, pp. 4–5.

2. Donald Lively, *The Constitution and Race*, New York: Praeger, 1992, p. 92.

3. Louis R. Harlan, "Desegregation in New Orleans Public Schools During Reconstruction," *American Historical Review*, 1962, 67:663–675.

4. Derrick Bell, *Race, Racism and American Law*, Boston: Little, Brown, 1973, pp. 445–448.

5. Samuel E. Morison, *The Oxford History of the American People*, New York: Oxford University Press, 1965, pp. 733–734.

6. Harvard Sitkoff, *The Struggle for Black Equality 1954–1992*, New York: Hill & Wang, 1993, pp. 4–5.

7. Lively, pp. 89–90.

8. Morison, p. 792.

9. Charles A. Lofgren, *The Plessy Case: A Legal-Historical Interpretation*, New York: Oxford University Press, 1987, p. 29.

10. 163 U.S. 537, p. 551.

11. *Ibid.*, p. 559.

12. Karl and Alma Taeuber, *Negroes in Cities: Residential Segregation and Neighborhood Change*, Chicago: Aldine, 1965, p. 3.

13. Sitkoff, p. 6.

14. Morison, pp. 793–794.

15. Langston Hughes, *Fight for Freedom: The Story of the NAACP*, New York: W. W. Norton, 1962, p. 24.

16. Booker T. Washington, *Up From Slavery*, New York: Lancer, 1968, p. 220.

17. Aldon Morris, *The Origins of the Civil Rights Movement: Black Communities Organizing for Change*, New York: Free Press, 1984, pp. 13–14.

18. Mary White Ovington, *How the National Association for the Advancement of Colored People Began*, New York: NAACP, 1914, p. 1.

19. Kimberly Lewis, *The NAACP Legal and Educational Fund, Inc., and the Civil Rights Movement*, New York, 1980, pamphlet, p.4.

20. 238 U.S. 347.

21. 245 U.S. 60.

22. 305 U.S. 337.

23. NAACP Legal Defense and Educational Fund, *Toward Equal Justice*, New York: NAACP, undated, p. 7.

24. Carter G. Woodson, *A Century of Negro Migration*, New York: Russell & Russell, 1969, p. 160.

25. John Hope Franklin and Alfred A. Moss, Jr., *From Slavery to Freedom: A History of Negro Americans*, New York: Knopf, 1987, p. 608.

26. Mark Tushnet, *The NAACP's Legal Strategy Against Segregated Public Education*, 1925-1950, Chapel Hill, NC: University of North Carolina Press, 1987, p. 105.

Chapter 3

1. Lisa Aldred, *Thurgood Marshall*, New York: Chelsea House, 1990, p. 28.

2. *Ibid.*, p. 31.

3. Tushnet, p. 45.

4. Lewis, p. 8.

5. Roger Goldman and David Gallen, *Thurgood Marshall: Justice for All*, New York: Carroll & Graf, 1992, pp. 93–94.

6. *McLaurin* v. *Oklahoma State Regents*, 339 U.S. 637, and *Sweatt* v. *Painter*, 339 U.S. 629.

7. *NAACP Annual Report*, 1950, New York: NAACP, 1951, pp. 7–8.

8. Loren Miller, *The Petitioners: The Story of the Supreme Court of the United States and the Negro*, New York: Pantheon, 1966, p. 336.

9. 339 U.S. 637.

10. Miller, pp. 338–339.

11. Aldred, p. 68.

12. 339 U.S. 629.

13. *Ibid.*

14. Philip Kurland and Gerhard Casper, *Landmark Briefs and Arguments of the Supreme Court of the United States: Constitutional Law*, (Trial Transcript, *Brown* v. *Board of Education*) Arlington, VA: University Publications of America, 1958, vol. 49, p. 285.

15. *Ibid.*, p. 290.

16. *Ibid.*, p. 301.

17. *Ibid.*, p. 293.

18. *Ibid.*, p. 310.

19. *Ibid.*, p. 316.

20. *Ibid.*, p. 318.

21. David Halberstam, *The Fifties*, New York: Villard Books, 1993, p. 416.

22. *Ibid.*, p. 420.

23. Goldman and Gallen, p. 102.

24. Kurland and Casper, vol. 49A, p. 1316.

Chapter 4

1. Kurland and Casper, vol. 49A, p. 546.

2. *Ibid.*,p. 556.

3. Aldred, p. 16.

4. William Henry Harbaugh, *Lawyer's Lawyer: The Life of John W. Davis*, New York: Oxford University Press, 1973.

5. William Henry Harbaugh, "John W. Davis," in Kermit L.

Hall, *The Oxford Companion to the Supreme Court of the United States*," New York: Oxford University Press, 1992, p. 219.

6. Kluger, p. 529.

7. Kurland and Casper, vol. 49A, p. 489.

8. Woodson, p. 160.

9. Kurland and Casper, p. 332.

10. *Ibid.*, p. 333.

11. *Barbier* v. *Connolly*, 113 U.S. 27.

12. Kurland and Casper, p. 432.

13. *Ibid.*, p. 491.

14. *Ibid.*, p. 339.

15. *Ibid.*, p. 340.

16. *Ibid.*, p. 334.

17. NAACP Legal and Educational Defense Fund, pp. 17–18.

18. Kurland and Casper, p. 297.

19. *Ibid.*, vol. 49A, p. 491.

20. *Ibid.*, p. 337.

21. *Ibid.*, p. 338.

22. United States Supreme Court, *Transcript of Oral Arguments*, No. 101, 1952, p. 113.

23. *Ibid.*, p. 118.

24. *Ibid.*, p. 86.

25. United States Supreme Court, *Transcript of Oral Arguments*, No. 8, 1952, p. 138.

26. *Ibid.*, p. 126.

27. Kurland and Casper, p. 341.

28. United States Supreme Court, *Transcript of Oral Arguments*, No. 101, 1952, p. 60.

29. Kurland and Casper, p. 336.

30. *Ibid.*, p. 429.

31. *Ibid.*, p. 340.

32. *Ibid.*, p. 522.

33. United States Supreme Court, *Transcript of Oral Arguments*, No. 101, 1952 p. 189.

Chapter 5

1. Halberstam, p. 413.

2. Tony Freyer, "Jackson-Black Feud," in Hall, 1992, pp. 445–446.

3. *Ibid.,* p. 445.

4. Walter F. Pratt, Jr., "Frederick Moore Vinson" in Hall, 1992, pp. 898–899.

5. Frankfurter Papers, Harvard University, cited in Bernard Schwartz, *Super Chief: Earl Warren and His Supreme Court, A Judicial Biography,* New York: New York University Press, 1983, p. 72.

6. William O. Douglas, *The Court Years, 1939-1975: The Autobiography of William O. Douglas,* New York: Random House, 1980, p. 113.

7. Fred Rodell, *Nine Men: A Political History of the Supreme Court of the United States from 1790 to 1955,* New York: Vintage, 1955, p. 252.

8. Leonard Baker, *Brandeis and Frankfurter: A Dual Biography,* New York: Harper & Row, 1984, p. 253.

9. G. Edward White, *Earl Warren: A Public Life,* New York: Oxford University Press, 1982, p. 176.

10. Schwartz, p. 89.

11. Robert H. Jackson Papers, Library of Congress, in David M. O'Brien, *Constitutional Law and Politics,* vol. 2, New York: W.W. Norton, 1991, p. 1311.

12. Baker, p. 479.

13. Halberstam, p. 416.

14. Jack H. Pollock, *Earl Warren: The Judge Who Changed America,* Englewood Cliffs, NJ: Prentice Hall, 1979, p. 158.

15. *Ibid.,* p. 157.

16. Earl Warren, *The Memoirs of Earl Warren,* New York: Doubleday, 1977, p. 276.

17. *Ibid.,* p. 4.

18. *Ibid.*

19. Schwartz, p. 97.

20. Warren, p. 277.

21. Schwartz, p. 22.

22. Pollack, p. 174.

23. Warren, p. 4.

Chapter 6

1. Kurland and Casper, vol. 49A, pp. 449–458.

2. *Ibid.*, pp. 459–462.

3. *Ibid.*, pp.466–467.

4. *Ibid.*, pp. 479–488.

5. *Ibid.*, p. 522.

6. *Ibid.*, p. 523.

7. *Ibid.*, pp. 534–535.

8. *Ibid.*, pp. 538–539.

9. Pollack, p. 174.

10. Schwartz, p. 94.

11. Kluger, pp. 695–696.

12. Warren, p. 3.

13. 347 U.S. 483.

14. *Ibid.*

15. *Ibid.*

16. *Ibid.*

17. *Ibid.*

18. *Bolling* v. *Sharpe,* 347 U.S. 497.

19. *Ibid.*

20. *The New York Times,* "40% of Public School Pupils in U.S. Are in Areas Where Laws Require Segregation," May 18, 1954, p. 21.

Chapter 7

1. *The New York Times,* May 18, 1954.

2. Frank B. Kent, Jr., "School Segregation Banned in Nation," *Washington Post,* May 18, 1954.

3. Chalmer M. Roberts, "South's Leaders Are Shocked at School Integration Ruling," *Washington Post*, May 18, 1954.

4. Robert C. Albright, "Southerners Assail High Court Ruling," *Washington Post*, May 18, 1954.

5. *Ibid.*

6. *Ibid.*

7. 349 U.S. 294

8. Kurland and Casper, Vol. 49A, pp. 1167–1168.

9. Brief for the United States. October Term 1954. No. 1, p. 19, p. 768.

10. *Virginia* v. *West Virginia*, 200 U.S. 1.

11. Tinsley E. Yarborough, "John Marshall Harlan II" in Hall, 1992, p. 365.

12. Schwartz, p. 118.

13. O'Brien, vol. 2, p. 1318.

14. Schwartz, p. 119.

15. 349 U.S. 294.

16. *Ibid.*

17. Reed Sarratt, *The Ordeal of Desegregation: The First Decade*, New York: Harper & Row, 1966 p. 1.

18. *Ibid.*, p. 5.

19. Sitkoff, p. 29.

20. J. Harvie Wilkinson III, *From Brown to Bakke: The Supreme Court and School Integration, 1954–1978*, New York: Oxford University Press, 1976, p. 91.

21. Miller, p. 357.

22. 358 U.S. 1.

23. Baker, p. 483.

24. *Shuttlesworth* v. *Alabama*, 358 U.S. 101.

25. Miller, p. 353.

26. *Griffin* v. *County School Board*, 377 U.S. 218.

27. Richard Polenberg, *One Nation Divisible: Class, Race, and Ethnicity in the United States Since 1938*, New York: Viking, 1980, p. 190.

28. P.L. 88–352, Title IV, #407, 1964, (a) (2).

29. See *Bradley* v. *Richmond School Board*, 382 U.S. 103; *Green* v. *County School Board*, 391 U.S. 430; and *U.S.* v. *Jefferson County School Board*, 372 F ed. 836.

30. Miller, p. 376.

31. Alois V. Adair, *Desegregation: The Illusion of Black Progress*, Lanham, MD: University Press, 1984, pp. 15, 31–32.

32. *Rodriguez* v. *San Antonio*, 411 U.S. 1.

33. U.S. Commission on Civil Rights, *Twenty Years After Brown*, Washington, DC: United States Government Printing Office, 1975, p. 167.

34. *Swann* v. *Charlotte-Mecklenburg Board of Education*, 402 U.S. 1.

35. Wilkinson, pp. 213–214.

36. *Milliken* v. *Bradley*, 418 U.S. 717.

37. *Ibid.*

38. Nathan Glazer, *Affirmative Discrimination: Ethnic Inequality and Public Policy*, New York: Basic Books, 1975, p. 123.

39. Diane Ravitch, *The Revisionists Revised: A Critique of the Radical Attack on the Schools*, New York: Basic Books, 1977, p. 106.

Glossary

amicus curiae—Someone who is not a party to a lawsuit but who has a point of view for the court to consider.

bill of attainder—An edict or law finding a person guilty of a crime without a trial; a common practice in England and the colonies before the Revolution, but prohibited by the Constitution.

brief—Written legal arguments presented by the parties to a lawsuit. They are written to persuade the court of a particular position.

class action—A lawsuit brought on behalf of a large group of people who all claim to have been wronged by the defendant in a similar way.

concurrence or **concurring opinion**—An opinion written by a judge who agrees with the decision of the court but disagrees with the reasons for the decision.

court—Judge or judges who sit and listen to arguments or write decisions are called "the court."

decree—An official order of the court.

defendant—The party in a lawsuit who is being sued. The other party in the case claims that they have been wronged by the defendant.

disenfranchise—To take away one's right to vote.

dissent or **dissenting opinion**—An opinion written by a judge who disagrees with the opinion of the majority of the court.

filibuster—A tactic used especially by United States Senators who are opposed to a bill. They speak so long during the debate that the bill in question never actually comes up for a vote.

grandfather clause—A state law about voting that said that everyone had to take a test in order to vote unless their grandfather had voted. It was designed to deny African Americans, whose grandfathers had been slaves, the right to vote.

Jim Crow Laws—Laws and customs in the South during the period of segregation that required separate facilities for blacks.

judicial activism—Making decisions that depart from precedent on the court and may lead to dramatic changes in the law.

judicial restraint—Following precedent set by the court and interpreting the law conservatively.

jurisdiction—The legal boundaries or limits of the court's power.

natural law—A belief that certain laws can be derived from nature, instead of or in addition to laws passed by a legislature.

opinion—A written explanation of a judge's decision discussing the legal precedents and the reasoning of the court.

oral argument—An opportunity for the parties to discuss their case with the court. Lawyers answer questions from the court and explain why their party should win.

parties—The two sides of a lawsuit.

plaintiff—The person or group of people who begin a lawsuit claiming that they have been wronged by the defendant.

police power—The power of the government to keep peace and protect public safety within the state.

political question—A decision that should be made by the legislative or executive branch of the government. Therefore, it is not proper for a court to make this decision.

poll tax—A method of keeping African Americans from voting by charging a tax in order to vote.

precedent—All of the prior decisions on an issue that is presently before a court. The court is supposed to decide a case in a way that is consistent with decisions that have come before it.

separate but equal—An interpretation of the Fourteenth Amendment first announced by the Supreme Court in an 1896 decision called *Plessy* v. *Ferguson.* It said that segregated facilities were not unconstitutional as long as they were not inferior for African Americans.

stare decisis—A principle of legal decision. It requires that a court's decision be consistent with precedent.

states' rights—An argument by the southern states stating that they had a great deal of power to make laws under the Tenth Amendment. It also said that the federal government had little control over education.

Further Reading

Adair, Alois V., *Desegregation: The Illusion of Black Progress*, Lanham, MD: University Press, 1984.

Aldred, Lisa, *Thurgood Marshall*, New York: Chelsea House, 1990.

Arbeitman, Lee and Richard L. Roe, *Great Trials in American History*, St. Paul, MN: West Publishing Co., 1985.

Baker, Leonard, *Brandeis and Frankfurter: A Dual Biography*, New York: Harper & Row, 1984.

Bell, Derrick, *Race, Racism and American Law*, Boston: Little, Brown, 1973.

Berman, Daniel M., *It Is So Ordered: The Supreme Court Rules on School Desegregation*, New York: W.W. Norton, 1966.

Blumberg, Rhoda L., *Civil Rights: The 1960s Struggle*, Boston: Twayne, 1991.

Douglas, William O., *The Court Years, 1939-1975: The Autobiography of William O. Douglas*, New York: Random House, 1980.

Franklin, John Hope, *From Slavery to Freedom: A History of Negro Americans*, New York: Knopf, 1987.

Glazer, Nathan, *Affirmative Discrimination: Ethnic Inequality and Public Policy*, New York: Basic Books, 1975.

Goldman, Roger and David Gallen, *Thurgood Marshall: Justice for All*, New York: Carroll & Graf, 1992.

Halberstam, David, *The Fifties*, New York: Villard Books, 1993.

Hall, Kermit L., *The Oxford Companion to the Supreme Court of the United States*, New York: Oxford University Press, 1992.

Harbaugh, William H., *Lawyer's Lawyer: The Life of John W. Davis*, New York: Oxford University Press, 1973.

Hughes, Langston, *Fight for Freedom: The Story of the NAACP*, New York: W.W. Norton, 1962.

Kluger, Richard, *Simple Justice: The History of Brown* v. *Board of Education and Black America's Struggle for Equality*, New York: Knopf, 1987.

Kurland, Philip and Gerhard Casper, *Landmark Briefs and Arguments of the Supreme Court of the United States: Constitutional Law*, Arlington, VA: University Publications of America, 1958.

Lewis, Kimberly, *The NAACP Legal and Educational Fund, Inc., and the Civil Rights Movement*, New York: NAACP, 1980.

Lively, Donald, *The Constitution and Race*, New York: Praeger, 1992.

Lofgren, Charles A., *The Plessy Case: A Legal-Historical Interpretation*, New York: Oxford University Press, 1987.

Miller, Loren, *The Petitioners: The Story of the Supreme Court of the United States and the Negro*, New York: Pantheon, 1966.

Morison, Samuel E., *The Oxford History of the American People*, New York: Oxford University Press, 1965.

Morris, Aldon, *The Origins of the Civil Rights Movement: Black Communities Organizing for Change*, New York: Free Press, 1984.

NAACP Legal and Educational Defense Fund, *Toward Equal Justice*, New York: NAACP, undated.

O'Brien, David M., *Constitutional Law and Politics*, New York: W.W. Norton, 1991.

Ovington, Mary White, *How the National Association for the Advancement of Colored People Began*, New York: NAACP, 1914.

Polenberg, Richard, *One Nation Divisible: Class, Race, and Ethnicity in the United States Since 1938*, New York: Viking, 1980.

Pollock, Jack H., *Earl Warren: The Judge Who Changed America*, Englewood Cliffs, NJ: Prentice Hall, 1979.

Ravitch, Diane, *The Revisionists Revisited: A Critique of the Radical Attack on the Schools*, New York: Basic Books, 1977.

Rodell, Fred, *Nine Men: A Political History of the Supreme Court of the United States from 1790 to 1955*, New York: Vintage, 1955.

Sarratt, Reed, *The Ordeal of Desegregation: The First Decade*, New York: Harper & Row, 1966.

Schwartz, Bernard, *Super Chief: Earl Warren and His Supreme Court. A Judicial Biography*, New York: New York University Press, 1983.

Sitkoff, Harvard, *The Struggle for Black Equality 1954-1992*, New York: Hill & Wang, 1993.

Taeuber, Karl and Alma, *Negroes in Cities: Residential Segregation and Neighborhood Change*, Chicago: Aldine, 1965.

Tushnet, Mark, *The NAACP's Legal Strategy Against Segregated Education*, 1925-1950, Chapel Hill, NC: University of North Carolina Press, 1987.

Warren, Earl, *The Memoirs of Earl Warren*, New York: Doubleday, 1977.

Washington, Booker T., *Up from Slavery*, New York: Lancer, 1968.

White, G. Edward, *Earl Warren: A Public Life*, New York: Oxford University Press, 1982.

Wilkinson, J. Harvie III, *From Brown to Bakke: The Supreme Court and School Integration, 1954-1978*, New York: Oxford University Press, 1976.

Woodson, Carter, *A Century of Negro Migration*, New York: Russell & Russell, 1969.

Index

9/02